STONES AND BONES

OF NEW ENGLAND

A Guide to Unusual, Historic,
and Otherwise Notable Cemeteries

Lisa Rogak

The
Globe
Pequot
Press

GUILFORD, CONNECTICUT

Photo credits: pp. 1, 18 © Jack McConnell, www.mcconnellpix.com; pp. 4, 20, 21, 24, 26, 34, 42, 53, 55, 67, 70, 75, 85, 87, 96, 97, 104, 105, 110, 112, 114, 116, 118, 120, 126, 144, 153, 162, 167, 170, 173, 179, 189, 193, 195 (bottom), 199 courtesy The Association for Gravestone Studies; pp. 6, 8, 35, 40, 57, 59, 73, 92, 137, 146, 177, 195 (top) courtesy Library of Congress; pp. 130, 134 by Lisa Rogak

Text design: Lisa Reneson, TwoSistersDesign.com
Maps by Stefanie Ward © The Globe Pequot Press

Library of Congress Cataloging-in-Publication Data
Rogak, Lisa, 1962-
    Stones and bones of New England : a guide to unusual, historic, and otherwise notable cemeteries / Lisa Rogak. -- 1st ed.
       p. cm.
    Includes bibliographical references and index.
    ISBN 0-7627-3000-5
    1. Cemeteries--New England--Guidebooks. 2. Historic sites--New England --Guidebooks. 3. New England--Guidebooks. 4. New England--History, Local. I. Title.

F5.R64 2004
929'.5'0974--dc22

2004054201

Manufactured in the United States of America
First Edition/Second Printing

CONTENTS

Connecticut

Maine

Massachusetts

New Hampshire

Rhode Island

Vermont

INTRODUCTION

To know the character of a community,
I need only visit its cemeteries.

—BENJAMIN FRANKLIN

Taphophilia

My family has always had a thing for old cemeteries. Before I moved to northern New England years ago, if anyone asked why I wanted to live in such a godforsaken place, I usually replied, "To be near the history."

Truth be told, my answer should have been "To be near the old cemeteries." But I knew that not everyone shared my passion for old burial grounds. To me, though, cemeteries are a chronicle of past lives and events presented with some great old art. Who needs a history book when all you have to do is walk through the gate of an old New England graveyard—still used or not—where you can read the inscriptions, wonder about the lives of the people who lie beneath your feet, and imagine yourself back in their shoes and their century?

Maybe it's a genetic thing. I remember seeing photographs of my parents on their honeymoon. Where were they standing? In Vermont, next to an old cemetery.

My mother once told me that her own mother used to take her kids on Sunday strolls through the local cemetery in Elizabeth, New Jersey, and point to the less and more desirable sections, much the way a real estate agent today would point out the better neighborhoods on a house-hunting drive.

"Don't bury me over there," my grandmother would say, pointing to a swampy area on the western side of the cemetery. "It floods." *No problem with that,* I thought; *she doesn't want to spend eternity in a waterlogged casket.* That wasn't the entire story, however. I later discovered that to Polish people, water in the grave means that the one lying there in death was a chronic drunk in life.

Today the town I live in—Grafton, New Hampshire—has a total of fourteen cemeteries, as recorded by the New Hampshire Old Cemetery Association. Five are small family cemeteries on private land with only a few plots, while only one cemetery is still in use. Pretty remarkable for a town with a population of around 1,100, though in its heyday Grafton served as a stopover point on the Boston & Maine Railroad, with a peak population of 3,000 in 1850.

I pass by one of the older closed cemeteries several times a day, but there's a more intriguing "tombstone" right by the side of the road. No one is buried there; still, it commemorates an event that the survivors felt compelled to broadcast to future generations. About 0.2 mile up Kinsman Road on the left-hand side of the dirt road in Grafton is a simple marker that reads:

RUTH COLE
THROWN FROM THE WAGON AND KILLED
APR 28, 1863, AE 23 YRS 2 MO.

You might think that this was a warning against the evils of alcohol, but the story goes that Ruth Cole, the daughter of a farmer over on nearby Prescott Hill, traveled up Kinsman to see her fiancé. Once she arrived at his homestead, he informed her that he no longer wanted to marry. In her grief, she flew down Kinsman toward home in her wagon at great speed, and when she hit a rut in the road, she was thrown from the cart. She later died.

In the winter the road crew places a flag on the marker so it doesn't get hit by the snowplow. Someone from the historical society places a bouquet of plastic lilacs by the stone each April, or sometimes May. That's the sign to people on the road that spring is finally here. The blackflies inevitably show up in droves the next day.

I guess it was natural back then, in the days before virtual funerals and living memorials and online memorial services, to commemorate Ruth Cole's memory in a permanent way, and that was in the form of a tombstone. You'll discover that it's not unusual in New England to have a tombstone without a body. Numerous stories are told in this book, often of a long-ago tragedy where the body was lost but the memory wasn't, and the people yearned to explain the misfortune to future generations. Like I said, history on a tombstone.

There's a name for people who share my passion for cemeteries: The formal term is *taphophile,* which means "one who loves cemeteries." That passion develops for a variety of reasons. Some folks haunt burying grounds to learn about a particular town, while others use them as a quiet refuge in the summertime. Still others just love the feel of history that emanates from the stones. And there's a growing group of people who rely on cemeteries to conduct genealogical research, charting their family histories.

I'll never forget the time I stopped by the Village Cemetery in Woodstock, Vermont, a few years ago, with a couple of books and a bottle of water. I was all ready to snuggle up against my favorite tree for the afternoon when I saw it was already taken by someone who had the same idea. Ditto for the three or four other "favorite" trees I checked that day. I finally settled on an old wrought-iron fenced-in grave. In the future I visited cemeteries in less traveled towns.

Though it's best to physically experience an old cemetery, to walk its uneven earth and touch the rough granite, sometimes time or distance makes it impossible to visit an old New England graveyard that has particular meaning to you. No problem, for there's an online network of taphophiles on several Web sites—including Ancestry.com and Headhunters.net—where they can meet up and post queries and answer questions. For instance, someone in Kansas can post a request for a photo of the gravestone of an ancestor buried in a long-abandoned cemetery in Vermont's Northeast Kingdom region. Time and again, someone who lives there will volunteer for the job and traipse out to the tiny, remote graveyard, take a digital picture of the tombstone, and send it to the amateur genealogist as an e-mail attachment.

I'd bet that most of the people buried in these cemeteries would think this is just great.

The Mysteries of Old Cemeteries

Johnny Bassett, a longtime road agent (now retired) in my town of Grafton, New Hampshire, once told me a story about a town cemetery. In his job he was often called upon to help dig graves because of his experience in operating backhoes and other heavy equipment.

One day in the 1970s, he was asked to help dig a grave in one of the town graveyards that hadn't been used in a while. A longtime resident had just died; she had purchased her cemetery lot in the 1930s, before it had closed to new interments. Now, this was a small piece of land. Perhaps seventy-five graves and tombstones were placed there before space ran out and the cemetery was declared closed to new "users."

Johnny had the instructions for where the new grave should go—to the right of Mister Edwards's stone—so he steered the backhoe into the cemetery, over the bumpy hillocks and down the narrow paths, all without knocking any of the stones over. He located the approximate site where the new grave should go, and with the help of one of his assistants, he began to dig. A few feet down, the backhoe struck something. He thought it was just a boulder, so he moved the shovel at an angle to try to dislodge it. When he thought he had the shovel under the main heft of the rock, he lifted the crane—and the top of a casket popped off, revealing a very well-preserved Mister Edwards in his 1950s finery. John's assistant took one look and ran screaming down the road, not stopping until he reached his home a good 3 miles away.

Because cemetery records through most of New England's history were kept by hand, and usually in a faded, spidery script, it's inevitable that things were sometimes incorrect. In addition, in the days before the use of grave vaults was mandatory, decades of New England weather left their mark: Cemetery grounds tended to shift and buckle, and the caskets moved. Digging graves in the cemetery at least several times a year also tended to disturb the ground below.

To research a particular cemetery—or to get some idea of how many cemeteries there were and how populated a particular town was—get a gazetteer for your state. Better yet, get a reproduction of a town or county map from the late 1890s that lists the owners of all the homes in town by last name. There you'll usually see all the cemeteries in town—at a time when most were active—and receive clues as to where to look for them now. Keep in mind that some are now located in parts of a town where roads are no longer maintained by the municipal government, or perhaps in a part of town that is now totally uninhabited—a ghost town of sorts. One good source for town and county map reproductions is Old Maps of New York and New England at www.oldmapsne.com (335 Secret Lake Road, Athol, MA 01331-9579); you can also try checking with local or state historical societies.

Visiting an abandoned cemetery in an old New England town is one way to appreciate the often bustling history that's gone on before you. Many of these abandoned graveyards have a volunteer cemetery commissioner who makes sure the grass gets cut at least a couple of times each summer. But an abandoned cemetery in a place that is now nothing more than cellar holes and logging trails barely visible between the weeds and blown-down trees is truly a spooky experience. You can almost see the ghosts. In fact, as you'll read, some have. A couple of these ghost cemeteries are Bara-Hack Cemetery in Pomfret, Connecticut, and Laurel Hill Cemetery in Wilton, New Hampshire.

If you do choose to explore a cemetery in an abandoned village, remember that it is now private land, and watch for POSTED signs to make sure you're not trespassing. If you visit a cemetery that's listed as private in this book, it's necessary to first ask permission of the landowners before venturing onto the land.

All this is to let you know that cemeteries in New England will sometimes surprise you, and even though an old map or legend tells you one thing, or the cemetery superintendent swears to you that something is there, sometimes these old graveyards have a funny way of not being entirely what they seem. In some cases people who are supposed to be buried in one spot aren't there at all, while others are interred in the ground without a headstone or other marker, which was common during times of epidemics or a disaster like a shipwreck where the names of the deceased were simply not known. And then there are the burial yards that went unrecorded until a bulldozer breaking ground for new development made the discovery.

During pre-Revolutionary years, the colonists placed their graveyards close to town, next to church, where they could view them regularly and be reminded of their own mortality. Later on, as the population grew and spread out, many people preferred to bury their dead on their own land, for much the same reasons as their forebears. Today people have numerous choices when it comes to the disposal of their dead. It's an age of homogenized memorial parks, with strict rules about interment and the size and shape of stones, and it could well be that the ability to read an era's history from a walk through the cemetery is gone. All the more reason to take time to walk through the old graveyards.

If, like me, you've long appreciated New England's ancient burial grounds, you may be used to hearing "How morbid!" when you disclose your interest in all things cemetery-related, or that you're a taphophile. But you know the beauty, the history, the peace that old graveyards offer, and there are few places today where you can get all three in one place, and for free. You can't beat that.

How to Use This Book

In researching and writing this book, I made it a point to focus on the legends and the people buried in the cemeteries described, for good and bad. After all, without the great spooky stories and superstitious gossip that were as much a part of seventeenth-century New England as they are today's world, a cemetery would just be a bunch of stones and bones. And if you are any kind of taphophile, you know that they're much more than that.

So what you'll find here is a collection of New England cemetery highlights. These are the graveyards with the most interesting stories to tell, the most intriguing people to meet, the clearest glimpses—sometimes funny, sometimes poignant—of days gone by. I'll tell you where to find each of these unique burial grounds, and steer you toward some of their treasures. But I won't tell you all their secrets. The joy of poking around old graveyards is, well, poking around old graveyards. I don't want to spoil all their surprises for you.

Where there's a cemetery office, I'll let you know, and I'll give you their phone number and contact information. A lot of these cemeteries are less formal than that, of course; you'll want to explore them for yourself.

When you do, be sure to check out the information you'll find in the back of this book. I've included a list of some of the images commonly found on New England gravestones, along with their meanings. And I've explained all those mystifying abbreviations you'll often find on tombstones. No, they're not Latin. (Well, sometimes they are.) Finally, there's a list of good books to help you find out more, and a collection of New England taphophile resources to help you along the way.

So take some time to leaf through this book now. A certain cemetery or image of a stone may just inspire you to plan your next trip around a burying ground. If it does, by all means bring this book with you when traveling throughout New England.

Above all, when you visit the cemeteries described in this book, keep in mind that they are, after all, burying grounds where generations of people have said good-bye to their loved ones. Whether public or private, active or abandoned, quiet respect is the appropriate mode of behavior.

CONNECTICUT

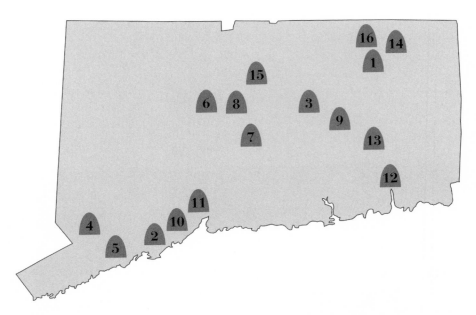

1   Ashford: Westford Hill Cemetery

2   Bridgeport: Mountain Grove Cemetery

3   Coventry: Nathan Hale Cemetery

4   Easton: Union Cemetery

5   Fairfield: Old Burying Ground

6   Farmington: Riverside Cemetery

7   Glastonbury: Green Cemetery

8   Hartford: Ancient Burying Ground

9   Mansfield: Mansfield Center Cemetery

10   Milford: Milford Cemetery

11   New Haven: Grove Street Cemetery

12   New London: Antientest Burial Ground

13   Norwich: Almshouse Cemetery

14   Pomfret: Bara-Hack Cemetery

15   Windsor: Palisado Cemetery

16   Woodstock: Woodstock Hill Cemetery

WESTFORD HILL CEMETERY

A Not-So-Frugal Yankee

ASHFORD

Public cemetery

*Near the meetinghouse on Westford Hill Road,
south of the intersection of Route 320.
Grounds open dawn to dusk.*

There's one or two in every old New England town. You know the type: the elderly women or men who dress in clothes that look like they're straight out of the 1920s, save every bit of aluminum foil and string they can get their hands on, and live in ramshackle houses that townspeople think should have been condemned long ago. And they would never think of spending a few of their precious pennies on a box of Girl Scout cookies, or doing some other good deed.

When they eventually die, however, it seems that no one is ever *really* surprised by the fact that these apparent eccentrics turn out to hold vast fortunes—which they've chosen to leave to the local animal shelter, or else they've blown it all on an elaborate 34-foot obelisk and painstakingly detailed grave plot that leaves everything else in the cemetery in the dust.

That's just what you'll find at the Westford Hill Cemetery in Ashford. Lucas Douglass was the stereotypical bitter old man; neighbor children always knew to cross the street rather than walk in front of his house. And he was such a miser that the town fathers figured they'd end up paying for his burial out of the town's pauper fund.

Instead, Mister Douglass surprised everyone after he died on December 5, 1895, on the main street of Ashford, dressed in rags and

Cemetery grounds tend to shift and buckle.

without a penny in his pocket. In his will he specified that the many thousands of dollars that comprised his estate go to build a veritable monument for his grave site. The obelisk you'll find in this cemetery today is made of marble imported from Italy and serves as the cornerstone of his final resting place. The site also features a handsome tombstone with a picture of the deceased, urns carved in stone, and a meticulously built stone wall that encases the entire plot. It figures that such an eccentric would be determined to have the last word.

Rest in Place

THE WORD *cemetery* COMES FROM THE GREEK, AND MEANS "SLEEPING PLACE."

MOUNTAIN GROVE CEMETERY

Final Home of P. T. Barnum
and Tom Thumb

BRIDGEPORT

Public cemetery

2675 North Avenue, off Exit 25 from I–95.
Grounds open 7:30 A.M.–6:30 P.M. Office hours:
8:30 A.M.–4:00 P.M. Monday–Friday. (203) 336–3579.
Map, pamphlets, and restroom available.

The first thing any visitor should know about Mountain Grove Cemetery is that P. T.—short for Phineas Taylor—Barnum is buried here. In fact, he designed the cemetery himself.

Bridgeport was Barnum's city. He was single-handedly responsible for the town's evolution from an important shipping hub into a vital East Coast manufacturing center as well—he used part of his vast circus fortune to improve the steamship industry, thereby improving Bridgeport. Barnum also served one term as mayor of Bridgeport, familiarly known as the Park City. In keeping with his outsized personality and accomplishments, some of the tombstones and monuments at this 140-acre cemetery are pretty elaborate. His own grave is marked by a towering granite monument with a series of granite steps to climb to reach it.

Tom Thumb, Barnum's most famous attraction, is buried right across from Barnum's grave. Born on January 4, 1838, Tom Thumb—whose given name was Charles S. Stratton—reached a height of 25 inches at one year of age before he stopped growing. Barnum discovered him when the boy was five years old and christened him Tom

A life-sized replica of Tom Thumb tops
the 40-foot obelisk honoring the 25-inch man.

Thumb. In 1863 Tom Thumb's wedding to Lavinia Warren, also a little person, was attended by 2,000 guests and was reported in newspapers across the country. He died in 1883 and was buried in Mountain Grove. The 40-foot obelisk that marks his grave has a life-sized marble replica of the little man perched on top. Some might think it ironic that this very tall monument was erected for one of the world's shortest men.

NATHAN HALE CEMETERY

He Gave His One Life

COVENTRY

Public cemetery

At the intersection of Routes 31 and 275, on Lake Street at the east end of Wangumbaug Lake. Grounds open dawn to dusk.

Every schoolchild knows that Nathan Hale said, "I only regret that I have but one life to lose for my country," in response to his capture by the British and subsequent execution. What most people probably don't know is that Hale was only twenty-one years old at the time of his death in 1776. His fate was sealed when he joined the Connecticut Militia to fight in the Revolutionary War, and the British captured him and sentenced him to hang for the crime of espionage—a charge that was never proven either way.

Nathan Hale was born in the town of Coventry, in the northeastern part of the state. And although his body still lies in an unmarked grave in Lower Manhattan where he was hastily buried after his execution, his family erected a special monument in the family cemetery back in Connecticut. The obelisk stands 45 feet high and is made from twenty-five tons of granite. Just off to the side of the monument you'll find the Hale family plot, with the original slate stone for Nathan and his brother, Richard, who also died and was buried elsewhere.

The family erected the monument in Nathan's memory in 1846, on the seventieth anniversary of his execution, and his famous words are inscribed on the base of the obelisk for all to see.

Revolutionary War hero Nathan Hale is remembered
with a 45-foot obelisk bearing his words "I only regret
that I have but one life to lose for my country."

UNION CEMETERY

Home of the White Lady

EASTON

Public cemetery

*At the junction of Stepney Road (Route 136) and
Sport Hill Road (Route 59), north of Exit 46 off
Route 15. Grounds open dawn to dusk.*

Union Cemetery has the dubious distinction of being one of Connecticut's most haunted sites—graveyard or not. The culprit is an apparition—also known as the "White Lady"—by the name of Mrs. Knox, who was reportedly murdered in the 1840s. The White Lady can be an extremely persistent ghost. Eyewitnesses say that she is always seen wearing a white nightgown with a bonnet on her head, and that she haunts not only one but two cemeteries: Union Cemetery in Easton and Our Lady of the Rosary Cemetery in nearby Monroe. Others report that she appears to be around thirty years of age with black hair. The only reported sightings have been at night, usually between two and three in the morning.

The White Lady doesn't restrict her appearances to the graveyards; she is frequently seen wandering the streets around the cemeteries. In fact, residents report that they have actually run over her with their cars—though she is usually seen back the next night, wandering aimlessly in her gown and bonnet. Mrs. Knox apparently has plenty of company, as local ghost chasers also tell of other ghostly figures, albeit darker and usually in shadow, trying to grab her between the tombstones in both cemeteries.

Locals also hold the White Lady responsible for several reports of peculiar behavior. Once, two children were killed in a car accident in front of the cemetery; on another occasion a woman suddenly began to attack her husband with a knife as they drove past. Another story blames the suicide of a young man—who used dynamite to blow himself up in front of the cemetery—on the White Lady.

I'll Cross That Bridge When I Get to It

IN OLD ENGLAND, IT WAS CONSIDERED A VERY DANGEROUS THING TO TAKE THE CORPSE TWICE ACROSS A BRIDGE FROM THE HOUSE WHERE THE DEATH HAD TAKEN PLACE—TO THE CHURCH AND BACK AGAIN TO THE BURIAL PLACE, FOR INSTANCE. IF THIS RULE SHOULD BE TRANSGRESSED, IT WAS THOUGHT THAT THE BRIDGE WOULD BREAK, SO IN ORDER TO AVOID SUCH A CATASTROPHE, CHAPELS WERE FREQUENTLY BUILT ON THE BRIDGE ITSELF.

—Bertram Puckle, *Funeral Customs*

OLD BURYING GROUND

The Mystery of the Two Wives

FAIRFIELD

Public cemetery

430 Beach Road, south of the town common.
Grounds open dawn to dusk.

Just when you think that all of Fairfield County has been paved over and built on, along comes a cemetery to remind you how very old this part of Connecticut is, and how much history abounds if you just look a little closer.

The Old Burying Ground in the town of Fairfield was established in 1687 and has obviously been very well kept and maintained over the years. More than one hundred soldiers from the Revolutionary War are buried here, in addition to one of Declaration of Independence signer John Hancock's aunts, by the name of Lydia Hancock.

In old New England cemeteries, you'll sometimes find a stone that presents a mystery that's never been solved. It can concern the dates of death or birth, the spelling of the family name, or even the question of whether a particular man was married to a particular woman. One of these mysteries shows up in the Old Burying Ground. Near the entrance to the cemetery, you'll find the grave for one Samuel Squier, who has what must have been a somewhat amusing epitaph for his time in the late eighteenth century:

> PRAISES ON TOMBSTONES ARE BUT VAINLY SPENT,
> ASSURED LIFE TO COME IS OUR BEST MONUMENT.

Next to Samuel's stone, you'll notice two tombstones for his wife, Mrs. Abigail Squier, an odd occurrence in itself. Occasionally, if a person who died had two stones, one would be in the place of death while the other was located in the town where he or she grew up, as a memorial stone. There would be no reason to have two stones for the same person right next to each other. But here they are.

The even stranger thing is that the dates of death and her age are different on each stone. On one, Mrs. Squier died in 1780 at the age of fifty-five, while the other reports that she died at fifty-two in 1785. The only explanation I can come up with is that Samuel married two different women named Abigail who died five years apart. And so far, no one in town has come up with a better explanation.

RIVERSIDE CEMETERY

Abolitionist History in the Graveyard

FARMINGTON

Public cemetery

*At the intersection of Maple Street and Garden
Street, 1 block west of Route 10.
Grounds open dawn to dusk.
(860) 674–0280.*

A handsome suburb of Hartford, Farmington is a picture-postcard old New England town, but its modern-day appearance hides a slice of African-American history in evidence at Riverside Cemetery.

Farmington was settled in 1640, but as was the case with much of New England, the land was home to numerous Native American tribes, some of whose names are long forgotten. Before Riverside Cemetery was set aside as the town's burial ground, it had served as a burial ground for the Tunxis tribe that occupied the region. As was the standard practice for the time, the white settlers assumed the burial ground as their own, eliminating any markers and signs of the previous users. Of course, most Indian tribes did not use markers for each grave, but they knew where everyone was buried, and the spot was sacred nonetheless. Today a small monument honors the memory of the tribe.

The other interesting piece of Farmington history is located along the main road that runs through the cemetery. Here you'll see a small stone plaque for a man by the name of Foone. The recent movie *Amistad* depicted the lives of Foone and his comrades, the native Africans who had sailed to America on a Spanish slave ship. When the ship was located near Farmington just off the coast, the slaves declared a mutiny and murdered several of the crew. In abolitionist New England, the townspeople of Farmington sympathized with the slaves and took them in. Court battles soon broke out between the United States and Spain over the cargo—human and otherwise—but the U.S. Supreme Court finally declared that the men were free citizens. They made plans to return to Africa, but in the meantime one of the slaves— Mister Foone—drowned while swimming in a local watering hole. Foone was buried in Riverside Cemetery; the following year, the rest of the men returned to Africa, leaving their comrade at rest in Connecticut.

GREEN CEMETERY

A Graveyard with Great Epitaphs

GLASTONBURY

Public cemetery

*On the town green, at the intersection of
Main Street and Hubbard Street.
Grounds open dawn to dusk.*

At first glance Green Cemetery appears to be as straightforward and
no-nonsense as its Puritan roots. The burial ground was established in
1692, and you can just imagine the reasoning: "It's on the green, so
we'll name it after the green."

Despite this stab at frugality, the epitaphs for some of the stones
are lyrical, poignant, and, in one case, quite lengthy.

First, the poignant. On the western edge of the cemetery, look for
a patch of reddish markers; they're made from red sandstone, a particularly porous material that has nonetheless stood up to the ravages of
time. On the stone for Marcy Halle, who died in 1719, the epitaph is
brief yet descriptive:

> HERE LIES ONE WHOSE LIFE THREADS
> CUT ASUNDER, SHE WAS STRUCKE DEAD
> BY A CLAP OF THUNDR.

Indeed, epitaphs can occasionally resemble news headlines. For
Deacon David Goodrich, part of the inscription on his slate stone reads:

. . . ON THE 7TH OF JUNE AD 1779 AT HIS EVENING PRAYER, FELL DOWN IN AN
INSTANT AND NEVER SAW TO MAKE ANY MOTION AFTER.

The wordiest example in the cemetery appears on the stone for Dr.
Elizur Hale, who died in 1790:

AT HIS DEATH ALL CLASSES PARTICIPATED IN THE DEEPEST
MOURNING, LAMENTING THE DEPARTURE OF THEIR PHYSICIAN
AND FRIEND. THE SAGE IS GONE . . .

The epitaph continues on for several more paragraphs.

ANCIENT BURYING GROUND

Hartford's First Cemetery

HARTFORD

Public cemetery

675 Main Street, just east of Bushnell Park.
Grounds open dawn to dusk.

Also known as the Center Church Graveyard, Hartford's Ancient Burying Ground was the first cemetery in what would become the state capital. Today the yard is not only the oldest historic site in the city but also the only site from the seventeenth century to remain intact.

From 1640, when the cemetery was established, to the early part of the nineteenth century, the Ancient Burying Ground was the only cemetery to be found within the city limits. Although it may appear that some of the brownstone markers from the cemetery's early decades are in great shape for their age, the truth is that they are reproductions of the early stones. The earliest extant example is the stone for Timothy Stanley, who died in 1648.

Hartford's first cemetery followed the custom of the day. The original settlers started with a small plot of land and then expanded it as need arose, but the process also worked in reverse: As government buildings and commercial developers in the city required more and more space, the older parts of the cemetery, with their weather-worn inscriptions and ill-maintained grounds—not to mention that the majority of grave sites had no stones to begin with—started to look pretty good. So although the church estimates that more than 6,000 people were buried in the Ancient Burying Ground over the years, today

In Hartford, as in many places, an entire modern city has sprung
up around old burial grounds.

the graveyard takes up four acres, with only 415 stones remaining.

Hartford in the late eighteenth and early nineteenth centuries had
a thriving community of free African Americans; custom dictated that
the community elect a "governor" to serve as an administrator and
maintain peace in the neighborhood. The Ancient Burying Ground
serves as the final resting place for five of these governors; the last governor, Boston Nichols, died in 1810 and in fact was one of the last people to be laid to rest in the cemetery.

In the Blink of an Eye

WELL—SICK—DEAD IN ONE HOUR'S SPACE.

—Epitaph for David Gardiner,
Ancient Burying Ground, Hartford, Connecticut

MANSFIELD CENTER CEMETERY

Art in Motion

MANSFIELD

Public cemetery

In the town center, on Route 195.
Grounds open dawn to dusk.

Looking at the faces carved on New England gravestones, it's hard not to notice the evolution of the stonecutters' art. The Old Cemetery in Mansfield Center provides a sort of walk through monumental history, with grave art ranging from highly stylized and sophisticated back to the cruder—some might even say cartoonlike—images of the distant past.

The Old Cemetery features a larger-than-usual number of old slate stones in remarkably good shape, given the fact that they date from the mid- to late 1700s. Take care to notice the stones in the Williams family plot; you'll see a veritable primer in carving styles through the centuries.

The Storrs family plot is located here as well—they founded the town of Storrs not far away. Note in particular the face on the stone for Olive Storrs, who died in 1785: She seems to register surprise, with large eyes and raised eyebrows. Similarly, the 1766 gravestone for Ruth Conant has a face that bears a strong resemblance to, well, Elmer Fudd.

In a more somber vein, carvers of the time occasionally liked to picture the deceased lying in his coffin, a design issue that presented a problem: How best to show the coffin and the body? A side view wouldn't work, and a full-body view was considered somewhat sacrilegious. This quandary explains why this image is so rarely seen on gravestones of the time. In the Old Cemetery, however, the stonecutter

The headstone for this 22-year-old, formerly in his "bloom of life," says: "I warn all friends, both old & young Not to live life as I have done."

who carved the 1768 stone for Bridget Snow accomplished the task in what was probably the best way possible: a view looking down at the deceased in the casket from above, with only the head showing. You can find the stone along the northern wall of the cemetery.

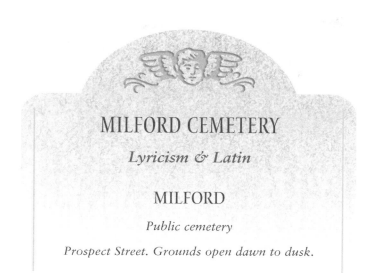

MILFORD CEMETERY

Lyricism & Latin

MILFORD

Public cemetery

Prospect Street. Grounds open dawn to dusk.

The best-known epitaph in Milford—or perhaps in all of Connecticut—can be found in Milford Cemetery. In the southeast corner of the cemetery, among a small group of very old sandstone and slate grave markers from the late eighteenth century, you can find the stone of Mary Fowler, who died in 1792 at the age of twenty-four.

> MOLLY THO PLEASANT IN HER DAY
> WAS SUDDENLY SEIZED AND SENT AWAY
> HOW SOON SHE'S RIPE HOW SOON SHE'S ROTTEN
> SENT TO HER GRAVE AND SOON FORGOTTEN

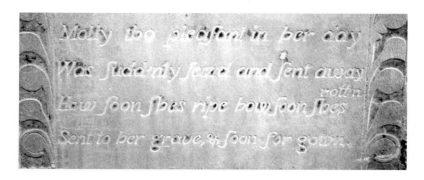

Molly's epitaph

In addition to Mary Fowler, Milford Cemetery serves as the final resting place for two colonial governors of Connecticut: Robert Treat, who helped to found the city of Newark, New Jersey, and died in 1710; and Jonathan Law, who died in 1750. A looming obelisk of red sandstone stands as a monument to a group of Revolutionary War soldiers who died of smallpox in 1777 along with Milford-born Captain Stephen Stow, who cared for them and subsequently died from the disease himself.

There's also the slate stone of the Reverend Whittelsey, died in 1768, whose inscription is written entirely in Latin. The adjacent red sandstone marking the grave for his son, who died in 1776, is written in English.

GROVE STREET CEMETERY

Final Resting Place for Eli Whitney
& Harriet Beecher Stowe

NEW HAVEN

Public cemetery

227 Grove Street, at High Street. The cemetery is
bounded by Tower Parkway on the south and
Prospect Street on the east; it's best reached by tak-
ing Exit 3 off I–91. Grounds open dawn to dusk.
(203) 787–1443.

For the most part, cemeteries established after the Revolutionary War developed in a haphazard fashion; most began as extensions of a churchyard, or as a public ground owned and managed by the town. Then, as they filled up, subsequent burials were placed wherever there was space, which sometimes required exhumation.

Grove Street Cemetery was an anomaly for its day, since from its first burial in 1796, future growth was planned out well in advance. The developers even went so far as to plan the width of the carriage lanes and their layout throughout the burial grounds. This was revolutionary for the time; parklike cemeteries such as Mount Auburn and Green-Wood in Brooklyn were still decades away from becoming reality. In a nod to these later rolling-hill cemeteries, however, the brownstone gates at the entrance to Grove Street were designed and installed in 1848, incorporating design elements of the Egyptian Revival style that was in vogue at the time.

The cemetery was in its infancy when the grand old patriots of the Revolutionary War started to die off. More than one hundred

The winged skull symbolizes flight of the soul from mortals;
the crown symbolizes the glory of life after death.

Revolutionary soldiers are buried here, along with an early president of Yale, Timothy Dwight; inventor Eli Whitney; and the father of Harriet Beecher Stowe. Just inside the gates is a legend to help visitors locate the more famous grave sites.

Grove Street also has some important "firsts" in its history: It was the first cemetery in the then-new nation to offer family plots to residents, and it was the first cemetery to incorporate, which also makes it one of the oldest corporations in the United States. Today the cemetery is maintained by Yale University; Yale Law School is adjacent to the graveyard. Grove Street was first called the New Burial Ground and consisted of only six acres. By the end of the 1800s, the cemetery had added six more acres to become the twelve-acre site it is today.

ANTIENTEST BURIAL GROUND

New London's Oldest Cemetery

NEW LONDON

Public cemetery

*Between Huntington Street and Hempstead Street;
the cemetery is bounded by Broad Street at the
northeast, just south of Route 85. Grounds open
dawn to dusk.*

The Antientest Burial Ground—also known as Antient and Antientist—
is the oldest cemetery in this very old Connecticut port town, which was
first settled in 1646. New London is rich in maritime history, and historians attribute its early development to the fact that it had very deep
water even up to the port, which facilitated navigation for the larger
ships of the day.

Though the last burial in Antientest occurred at least a couple of
centuries ago, the stones are in fairly good condition, considering the age
and the ravages that constant exposure to salt air can bring to a cemetery. Several prominent early residents of New London are buried here,
among them a Captain Richard Lord, who died in 1662 at the age of
fifty-two. Not only is Lord's one of the oldest stones in the cemetery, but
it has a curious inscription that starts out with the line "An epitaph on
Captain Richard Lord." Was it really necessary, I wonder, to spell out
the fact that we're reading an epitaph, given that we're standing in a
cemetery, and not in the town square reading the front page of the local
broadsheet newspaper? In any case, another feature of the stone is that
it lies flat and even with the ground, which of course is the custom in

Mr. Christopher Christophers died in 1687.

newer cemeteries to streamline maintenance, but it was extremely unusual back then.

Soldiers from the Revolutionary War are buried here as well, including Jonathan Brooks, who was referred to nationally as the boy patriot of the American Revolution. He died in 1848.

Sinking Stones

IN AN OLD CEMETERY, YOU MAY NOTICE THAT SOME OF THE STONES APPEAR TO HAVE SUNKEN. NEW ENGLAND'S GRAVEYARDS FREQUENTLY DATE FROM YEARS WELL BEFORE GRAVE VAULTS WERE MANDATORY IN MOST STATES. IN ADDITION, IN CROWDED CEMETERIES BODIES WERE ROUTINELY MOVED TO MAKE ROOM FOR MORE FAMILY MEMBERS. THIS RESULTS IN THE GRAVEYARD AND STONES LOOKING ASKEW, AND MAKES THE GROUNDS VERY DIFFICULT TO MAINTAIN.

ALMSHOUSE CEMETERY

Burial Site of the Poor Farm

NORWICH

Public cemetery

Follow Asylum Street north from Route 82. The cemetery is at the corner of Asylum Street and Alms House Lane. Grounds open dawn to dusk.

Not many of the people who pass through the town of Norwich, a well-preserved, well-kept city, would realize that in the nineteenth century, like many other towns its size, Norwich had a sizable poor farm, or "almshouse," located within its city limits.

Today it's primarily the state and federal governments that take care of those who have fallen down on their luck, but in the early years of the nation, it was the responsibility of each town government to take care of their own. Back then, they didn't do it with food stamps and supplementary rent money; the common method was to set aside a plot of land within the town where all the destitute—as determined by the town fathers—could live together as economically as possible, while giving them enough land to use so they could help themselves by growing their own food.

In Norwich, though public records show that town aid was given out as early as 1658, the first almshouse was not constructed until 1790. The cost to maintain it was too much for the town to bear, so a smaller almshouse was built on the town's main street to house the poor and indigent. It wasn't long, however, until the neighbors began to complain about the residents of the house. Whether they found the behavior of the people to be offensive, or the mere presence of the house reminded them that they could be living there themselves someday, is unclear. In any case, a third location for the almshouse was secured, this one away from the main business district on the north side of town. During the Civil War, the population of the house tripled due to the declining economic conditions.

Eventually, of course, the need arose to bury the house's residents. Given the local reaction to the earlier location of the house, government officials must have anticipated that taxpayers wouldn't want residents of the almshouse to be buried in any of the town cemeteries, either. So a graveyard was constructed adjacent to the almshouse. Today both the house and the cemetery are gone, but you can find a memorial marker in its place, honoring

THE 212 MEN, WOMEN AND CHILDREN WHO LIVED AND DIED
AT THE NORWICH ALMS HOUSE AND WERE LAID
TO REST HERE BETWEEN APRIL 21, 1888 AND JULY 12, 1927.

BARA-HACK CEMETERY
A Ghost Town Graveyard

POMFRET

Private cemetery

*From Route 44, head north on Route 97 for about
0.5 mile to a dirt road north of Mashamoquet Brook
on the left side of the road. Turn left onto this road
and continue for about 0.5 mile to reach Bara-Hack.
Grounds open dawn to dusk.*

Residents and visitors alike are always surprised to discover that overdeveloped parts of Connecticut boast numerous abandoned industrial sites—mills, mines, and the like—and even a ghost town or two, complete with cemetery. Bara-Hack, which means "breaking bread" in Welsh, is one of these little-known places. It was eventually incorporated into Pomfret Township.

Though the settlement was never what anyone would have referred to as bustling, even back in its early-nineteenth-century heyday, the number of stones in the cemetery attests to a thriving village where families named Randall and Higgenbotham predominated. The families were of Welsh descent and came to Connecticut by way of Cranston, Rhode Island. Though numerous parapsychologists and ghost chasers today visit the abandoned town and graveyard to witness the images and sounds of former villagers, the hauntings supposedly began shortly after the first residents were interred in the cemetery in the early 1800s. Maybe they were scared away, because by the time the Civil War rolled around, Bara-Hack was uninhabited.

Then, as now, visitors to the town and cemetery reported hearing children's voices, livestock, and dogs, as well as the occasional sound of a wagon passing by in broad daylight. Some even tell of seeing a baby reclining in the branches of an elm tree in the northern part of the cemetery.

In any case, researchers offer a variety of theories about why this particular burying ground seems particularly spooked, ranging from a murder among the town's early residents to an angry ghost. Though Bara-Hack is one of many allegedly haunted graveyards throughout the state, the fact that today it is part of a bona fide ghost town makes it an irresistible place to visit.

PALISADO CEMETERY

*Oldest (Legible) Gravestone
in Connecticut*

WINDSOR

Public cemetery

*75 Palisado Avenue. The cemetery is behind the First
Church, 0.5 mile north of the intersection with
Route 75. Grounds open dawn to dusk.*

Windsor, which is just north of Hartford, nestles against the Connecticut River. It was one of the first towns to be settled in Connecticut, and many of those early settlers are buried in Palisado Cemetery.

Unlike many other cemeteries that date from the mid-seventeenth century, Palisado is unique in that several of the oldest stones are still extant and readable, and they're not duplicates or reproductions. In fact, the oldest date said to be legible on a stone in any New England cemetery is at Palisado Cemetery, and belongs to the Reverend Ephraim Huit, who died in 1644. Likewise, the epitaph that appears on his stone is probably the oldest in the country as well, since epitaphs didn't start to appear on gravestones with any regularity until the 1800s. After all, in the earliest days of settlement in the New World, there was much to be done to establish a family homestead while simultaneously founding a town; who had the time or money to commission a tombstone with anything other than the basics, the name of the deceased and the dates of birth and death?

This tradition was obviously set aside for prominent citizens and men of the cloth, as the Reverend Huit's stone shows:

SOMETIMES TEACHER TO THE CHURCH OF WINDSOR,
WHO WHEN HEE LIVED, WE DREW OUR VITALL BREATH;
WHO WHEN HEE DYED, HIS DYING WAS OUR DEATH.

Another stone to check out in Palisado Cemetery is the one for Dr. Timothy Mather, who died in 1788, supposedly one of the largest markers made from red sandstone in all of New England.

WOODSTOCK HILL CEMETERY

Tempus Fugit

WOODSTOCK

Public cemetery

*Route 169, next to the First Congregational Church
off the green. Grounds open dawn to dusk.*

Strolling through modern cemeteries with their newer stones, it's exceedingly rare to find a gravestone that clearly reflects the personality of the deceased. Although in some places, people are choosing to have everything from motorcycles to palm trees inscribed on their stones or have a color photograph permanently sealed into the marble, sadly many new cemeteries are turning into the equivalent of community associations, with strict rules and no deviations. Of course, many of these newer graveyards require their stones to be no larger than a brick and flush with the ground, to facilitate maintenance. And there's little room on these tiny monuments to be creative.

In many New England cemeteries, happily, the tombstones can be as quirky as their owners and still as personalized as the stones centuries ago. In the Woodstock Hill Cemetery, the polished granite stone for Ethal Barrett, who died in 1941, features a cameo of the man with a dog, a rifle, and a fox. The epitaph:

> THIS IS FANNY, MY FAVORITE FOX HOUND.
> I HAVE SHOT OVER TWO HUNDRED FOXES
> WITH THE GUN THAT I HOLD.

If only everyone could be so sure of the message they want to leave behind to the world. And there's another stone that's equally famous at Woodstock Hill, but it's a lot older and just as rare as Ethal Barrett's.

A slate grave marker dating from 1752 contains a symbol that was highly unusual for its time: A clock was inscribed on the top of the stone. Given its composition, it is still in remarkably good shape. In those days, while clocks were becoming prevalent in colonial society, hourglasses were still the preferred method of showing the passage of time on tombstones. The hands on this carved clock point to XII and VI, the equivalent of the last grains of sand passing from the top half of the hourglass.

Sheaves of wheat symbolize the divine harvest.

Maine

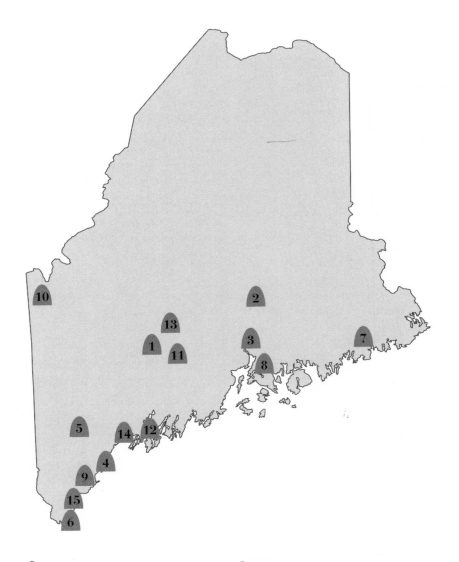

1 Augusta: State of Maine Burial Ground

2 Bangor: Mount Hope Cemetery

3 Bucksport: Buck Cemetery

4 Freeport: Webster Road Cemetery

5 Gray: Gray Cemetery

6 Kittery Point: Old Burying Yard

7 Machias: O'Brien Cemetery

8 North Brooklin: Brooklin Cemetery

9 Portland: Eastern Cemetery

10 Rangeley: Orgonon

11 Togus: Togus National Cemetery

12 Waldoboro: Old German Church and Cemetery

13 Winslow: Fort Hill Cemetery

14 Wiscasset: Ancient Cemetery

15 York: Old Burying Yard

STATE OF MAINE BURIAL GROUND

The Pine Tree State's
Little-Known Cemetery

AUGUSTA

Public cemetery

The capitol is just west of Route 201 on State House Street. Look for the burial ground on the eastern side of State House Park, just across from the capitol. Grounds open dawn to dusk.

This site is variously known in different sources as the State Capitol Grounds, the State House Park, and the State of Maine Burial Ground, which happens to be the oldest name. Though plenty of governors and other state dignitaries are buried in simple graveyards throughout the state, four are buried right on the capitol grounds in a plot on the far eastern side of the park.

The first burial of a high official here was for Enoch Lincoln, the third governor of Maine—after it separated from the Commonwealth of Massachusetts in 1820—who hailed from a family of governors, including his father and brother. Lincoln died while serving in his third term as governor in 1829. It wasn't until 1842 that the legislature approved funding to pay for a monument over Lincoln's grave.

Joshua Cushman, who died in 1834 and was interred in the State Burial Ground, served both state and towns in a governmental capacity for many years. He spent three years as a soldier in the Revolutionary War, after which he attended Harvard and graduated in 1788. He held a variety of elected offices, including both state representative and senator to the commonwealth, until his death at the age of seventy.

Two other early Pine State government officials were buried in the State of Maine Burial Ground—William Delesdernier, a state senator, and Charles Waterhouse, a clerk for the Maine house of representatives—but Governor Lincoln's was actually the last interment, in 1842. Today few people know that this quiet graveyard with but four markers even exists in the shadow of the statehouse.

MOUNT HOPE CEMETERY

Bangor's Garden Cemetery

BANGOR

Public cemetery

1048 State Street (Route 2). Grounds open dawn to dusk. Office hours: 7:30 A.M.–4:30 P.M. Monday–Friday. (207) 945-6589.

When Mount Auburn Cemetery in Cambridge, Massachusetts, was first designed, cities all throughout New England—and indeed the country—believed that having a garden cemetery in their city would be the saving grace for their own metropolis. The people of Bangor thought the same thing, and Mount Hope was their version of the Cambridge masterpiece.

Perhaps it was the much longer winters in Maine, or maybe it was the sparse population, but Mount Hope was never quite able to match its model in either size or detail. Still, it's worth a visit to view the graves of several prominent citizens here.

Northern Maine was—and still is—built on the backs of loggers. Since the earliest days of logging in the North Woods, amateur tinkerers have tried to come up with methods or tools to solve the many thorny problems peculiar to their specific line of work. The primary danger in the trade was the logjams. When shipping mammoth logs downriver, frequently some would get stuck, creating a huge pileup, disrupting the delivery, and damaging the shoreline. The usual solution was to send a man out on top of the logs to dislodge the jam, but this technique often resulted in the death of the man doing the job.

The tomb of Hannibal Hamlin, who served as
vice president under Abraham Lincoln

In 1858 a twenty-year-old blacksmith from Bangor named Joseph
Peavey invented a piece of equipment that allowed a logger to unlock
the logs while standing on shore; the tool soon came to be called a
peavey, and it turned out to be the most prized possession in a logger's
tool belt. Peavey died in 1918, and an image of his logjam tool appears
on his headstone.

Another famous resident buried in Mount Hope is Hannibal
Hamlin, who served as a congressman, senator, Maine governor, and
finally vice president under Abraham Lincoln. His tomb looms over the
graveyard, and at the time of his death in 1891, his funeral was supposedly the largest held in the state of Maine up until that time.

BUCK CEMETERY

The Cursed Leg

BUCKSPORT

Public cemetery

Main Street, just east of the Verona Bridge.
Grounds open dawn to dusk.

How would you like it if your town was most famous for—of all things—one part of a leg that involves an ancient witch's curse?

The town of Bucksport, near Bangor, has lived with just this notoriety since 1795, when a man known as Colonel Jonathan Buck—the town was named after him—died and was buried in the town cemetery, which was also named after the colonel. Buck, who served as a judge both in Bucksport and previously in his hometown of Haverhill, Massachusetts, was known as a stern taskmaster, even by eighteenth-century standards. Before he headed north to found the town that bears his name, Buck served on a trial in Massachusetts where he accused a woman of practicing witchcraft. She was found guilty, and he sentenced her to death by hanging.

On the day of the execution, just before the trapdoor was released, the woman placed a curse on the judge, announcing that she would dance on his grave. No one thought anything of it until after Buck died and a great marble obelisk was set to mark his grave up north in Bucksport. Shortly after the stone was set on top of his grave, a shadow in the shape of a woman's leg appeared on part of the stone. The townspeople thought somebody was playing a joke on them, and they proceeded to scrub away the mark. It didn't work. Then they tried to

A marble obelisk honors Colonel Jonathan
Buck, for whom Bucksport is named.

sand it away, and though the leg initially disappeared, it soon became
visible again in the same place on the stone. They tried numerous reme-
dies, and even though some may have initially appeared to be success-
ful, the imprint of the leg always came back in the same exact place.

Even today.

WEBSTER ROAD CEMETERY

The Final Resting Place of L.L. Bean

FREEPORT

Public cemetery

*From Route 1 North, turn left onto Desert
Road, and proceed for 2 miles to Webster Road;
the cemetery is 1 mile from the turn.
Grounds open dawn to dusk.*

In a simple game of word association, if you utter "Maine" to someone out west who's never visited the state, chances are he'll respond either with "lobster" or "L.L. Bean."

Today visitors to the state treat the main company store in Freeport as a kind of shrine to everything Maine. It's open twenty-four hours a day, and many travelers think that the only reason to come to Maine is to visit the store—oh, and eat a lobster.

If you count yourself in this category and feel that strongly about the store and its heritage, you should head a few miles out from the center of Freeport to view the grave site of Leon Leonwood Bean, the founder of the L.L. Bean empire, who died in 1967. His business philosophy was simple: "Sell good merchandise at a reasonable profit, treat your customers like human beings, and they'll always come back for more." So ingrained into the main workings of the company was Leon's motto that it's somewhat of a surprise to see that it doesn't appear on his headstone at Webster Road Cemetery, a small, peaceful graveyard on the periphery of Freeport. On the other hand, maybe it's more in keeping with his simple beliefs that only his name and dates of birth and death are inscribed on the small marker flush with the ground.

In fact, more people should run their businesses the way Leon Bean did. He founded his company with only one product, a pair of duck boots, which combined a rubber sole with a leather top that he designed himself. The first pairs that sold were defective, so Leon refunded the customers' money, tinkered with the design, and then proceeded to guarantee every purchase to every customer.

Today Freeport is a bona fide attraction for avid shoppers, and the town developed as a retail destination in large part due to the presence of the L.L. Bean store. Leon may not recognize the town today, but he'd recognize the quality that still permeates the company he made famous.

GRAY CEMETERY

Grave of the Unknown Confederate

GRAY

Public cemetery

Main Street, behind the firehouse.
Grounds open dawn to dusk.

In current times we look back at precomputer days and wonder how anything involving logistics ever got accomplished. Especially during wartime, when bodies had to be identified—sometimes an impossible task—and tagged and shipped back to the family on railroad cars, it's a wonder that the majority of families received their loved ones. But they did.

So in the 1860s, in the depths of the Civil War, when a body was rerouted incorrectly, it obviously stood out. This was the case in 1862 when a coffin bearing a body with no identifying marks except for a uniform arrived in the small town of Gray, Maine, straight from the battlefields of the South.

The townspeople who met the shipment had expected the coffin to contain the body of a local soldier, but to their great surprise, they found it was instead a deceased Confederate soldier. The women had no clues to the identity, and despite the great animosity between the Union and the Confederacy, they still believed that the man deserved a respectful and dignified burial.

They erected a plain marble tombstone in the town cemetery with the following inscription:

STRANGER, A SOLDIER OF THE LATE WAR DIED 1862,
ERECTED BY THE LADIES OF GRAY.

Each Memorial Day, the grave site is treated like that of any other veteran's, with one small exception: Instead of an American flag on the grave, a small Confederate flag flies.

OLD BURYING YARD

The Raging Sea

KITTERY POINT

Public cemetery

Route 103, across from the Congregational Church.
Grounds open dawn to dusk.

Today Kittery is best known for its outlet malls and traffic jams. Out at Kittery Point, however, the crowds thin out a bit: Shopping opportunities are pretty scarce at a cemetery.

Given that the early days of Kittery revolved around its coastline location, it's fitting that many of its tombstones from the nineteenth century and earlier tell stories of tragedy from the sea. One such stone in the southwest corner of the cemetery is for Margaret Hills, who died in 1803 at the age of twenty-eight. The epitaph reads:

> I LOST MY LIFE IN THE RAGING SEAS
> A SOV'REIGN GOD DOES AS HE PLEASE
> THE KITTERY FRIENDS THEY DID APPEAR,
> AND MY REMAINS, THEY BURIED HERE.

Another stone with a striking story to tell, along with an image, is a black slate marker—probably a reproduction—with a bronze plaque that shows an engraving of a ship in peril at sea. If you examine the plaque closely, you'll see a tiny sailor on the deck of the ship that's about to be broken to pieces. The epitaph on the stone reads:

BRIG HATTIE EATON, W.I. TO BOSTON
CAST AWAY ON GERRISH ISLAND MCH 21, 1876
CREW OF 8, WHITE AND NEGRO, AND 1 STOWAWAY.
NEAR THIS STONE LIE SIX BODIES NEVER CLAIMED.

The Walking Dead

POOR MARTHA SNELL, HER'S GONE AWAY,
HER WOULD IF HER COULD, BUT HER COULDN'T STAY.
HER HAD TWO BAD LEGS AND A BADISH COUGH,
BUT HER LEGS IT WAS THAT CARRIED HER OFF.

—Epitaph in a Bangor, Maine, cemetery

O'BRIEN CEMETERY

Resting Place of the Soldiers
of the First Naval Battle
of the American Revolution

MACHIAS

Public cemetery

Elm Street, just east of Route 1.
Grounds open dawn to dusk.

Washington County, where the town of Machias is located, is the last county in Maine before you run square into New Brunswick, Canada. This Down East enclave has a bit of history of which few are aware: Back in 1775 it was the site of the first naval battle in the war that we would come to know as the American Revolution.

Because this was serious logging country, the Battle of the *Margaretta* started over lumber in the same way that a later revolt in Boston began over tea. The Machias River runs through the town and offers a direct water route to transport logs from Machias to Boston. The British needed to build more barracks in Massachusetts to strengthen their military against the impending war, and so ordered the people of the town to send down some logs.

Tempers had been simmering for several years at that point between the colonists and the British, so the townspeople put their foot down and flatly refused to provide the timber.

Word of the rebellion quickly traveled. Soon a British schooner named the *Margaretta* was headed north up the river toward the town to squelch the uprising. Two local men who spearheaded the Mainers' effort, Jeremiah O'Brien and Benjamin Foster, planned an attack on the ship; other colonists agreed to back them up. When the ship arrived in town, the men from Machias launched their attack. They killed the captain of the ship and claimed it for their side. This battle, combined with other acts of rebellion occurring farther south in Lexington and Concord, Massachusetts, provided the first sparks to the tinderbox that would turn into the American Revolution.

O'Brien—the cemetery was later named after him—went on to have an illustrious political career as a result of his reputation for bravado. He served in both houses of the Maine legislature and was a U.S. congressman in the 1820s. He is buried here.

BROOKLIN CEMETERY

Grave Site of E. B. White

NORTH BROOKLIN

Public cemetery

*Route 175 and Cemetery Road, south of
Dog Wharf Road. Grounds open dawn to dusk.*

If you've ever loved the story of *Charlotte's Web* or *Stuart Little*, and you're going to be this far Down East in the state of Maine, you might as well pay a visit to the grave site of the author of these beloved children's books, E. B. White. He's buried in a small village cemetery in the little North Brooklin on the Blue Hill Peninsula.

While many are familiar with White's children's books, most aren't aware that he wrote for adults as well. He wrote for the *New Yorker* magazine for more than five decades, and he also frequently wrote stories about life on the small North Brooklin farm that he and his wife moved to in 1938. Their home on the peninsula is an area of salt marshes and small subsistence farms where hilly two-lane roads weave back and forth between the older, salt-bitten Capes. White liked to populate his stories—true and fictionalized—with scenes from this landscape, including the old rugged village and family cemeteries where the tombstones tilt toward each other in the crater-pocked graveyard.

The Brooklin Cemetery is pretty standard as far as small-town New England graveyards go, but the graves of White and his wife stand apart from the others. They're found toward the back of the cemetery, as if they're still somewhat off to the side, observing the goings-on in front of them. The two maple trees that hover over the Whites' stones were planted by friends in their memory.

EASTERN CEMETERY

Burial Place of
Lieutenant Henry Wadsworth

PORTLAND

Public cemetery

Congress Street and Washington Avenue, north of
Route 1A. Grounds open dawn to dusk.

Some say that Eastern Cemetery has the best view of the harbor of any graveyard in Portland. Actually, there are several cemeteries throughout New England where the same could be said of the town they're located in, but the history of this old port city, founded in the seventeenth century, makes Eastern Cemetery one of the richest, especially considering the naval military battles that have taken place here.

At the cemetery office, ask for directions to the Wadsworth monument, a white marble obelisk that marks the grave of one of Henry Wadsworth Longfellow's uncles: Lieutenant Henry Wadsworth, a naval officer killed in battle at the age of twenty. A fascinating story involves several graves adjacent to Wadsworth's, brick tombs with marble slabs on top, two with the same date of death. During the War of 1812, William Burrowes was commander of the U.S. ship *Enterprise,* while Samuel Blyth headed up the British counterpart, the *Boxer.* The ships engaged in a furious battle far out to sea; both commanders were killed, and the *Boxer* sank. The *Enterprise* headed for Portland bearing the captured British crew and the bodies of the deceased. The commanders were buried side by side in Eastern Cemetery along with a third—Kervin, a Portland boy also killed on the

Stately mausoleums stand side by side
along a well-trod path.

ship, who lies buried in the third of the brick tombs in the row.

In fact, Longfellow, who grew up in Portland, later memorialized the commanders and the battle in the poem "My Lost Youth."

The graves of two warring ship commanders
from the War of 1812

ORGONON

Wilhelm Reich's Estate
& Final Resting Place

RANGELEY

Public tomb

From Route 4, take Dodge Pond Road 4 miles from
the town center. Grounds open July and August,
Wednesday–Sunday 1:00–5:00 P.M.; September,
Sunday only 1:00–5:00 p.m. (207) 864-3443;
www.wilhelmreichmuseum.org.

While you may have heard of Dr. Wilhelm Reich, you may not have heard of his invention known as the Orgone, unless you were partaking in various activities popular in the 1960s.

Though Dr. Reich, an esteemed Austrian psychiatrist and a peer of Sigmund Freud, died in 1957, his ideas and inventions lived on just in time to hit the hip wave of the 1960s. Reich believed in the theory of Orgone Energy, whereby a special brand of physical energy is available to everyone universally that can provide us with boundless amounts of stamina, if only we can harness it from the air around us. Dr. Reich invented a device known as an Accumulator, which supposedly collected and concentrated the particles of Orgone Energy that were floating in the atmosphere. The idea was for a person to enter the machine, about half the size of a standard telephone booth, receive a large dose of Orgone, and have boundless amounts of energy.

He conducted most of his experiments in a laboratory at a lush mountaintop estate in Rangeley that he christened Orgonon, and he proceeded to market the Accumulator and other devices associated

Dr. Wilhelm Reich's grave can be found at
Orgonon's point of highest altitude.

with Orgone Energy. The Food and Drug Administration got wind of
Dr. Reich's efforts, labeled him a quack and a fraud, and gave him a
prison sentence that started in 1956. He died in a Lewisburg,
Pennsylvania, federal prison the following year, and his body was
shipped back to Rangeley for burial. The tomb has a bronze bust of Dr.
Reich on top, and it is specifically located at the point of highest altitude in the entire estate; perhaps the higher the altitude, the easier it is
to attract Orgone Energy?

TOGUS NATIONAL CEMETERY

Maine's Military Cemetery

TOGUS

Military cemetery

Hallowell Road, west of Route 226 and south
of the intersection of Routes 226 and 17.
Grounds open dawn to dusk.

Togus is the only national cemetery devoted to veterans in the state of Maine. Though today it is inactive, it is well maintained by the Veterans Administration and part of a regional VA center, including a medical center and a regional office (1 VA Center, Togus, ME 04330). The cemetery has just over 3,400 burials.

Togus is a derivative of *Worromontogus*, a Native American word that means "mineral water." In the mid-nineteenth century a summer resort occupied the land, which was owned by a wealthy investor named Horace Beals, from Rockland. At the time, hotels and resorts near natural mineral springs were popping up all over New England; people came to relax and drink the mineral water, which was supposed to have special health-giving properties even though it mostly smelled like rotten eggs, due to the high sulfur content.

Beals had elaborate plans to turn Togus into a mineral springs facility to rival Saratoga Springs in New York State, a place where tourists could come to watch horse races and "take the waters." His timing could have been better. After the Civil War began, people cut way back on travel. Togus, known as "Beals' Folly" by the locals, closed in 1863, and the federal government bought the property and

Veterans from the War of 1812 through the Vietnam War
are buried at Togus.

converted it to a residence for disabled soldiers as well as a veterans cemetery shortly after the end of the War Between the States.

Today the Togus National Cemetery contains the graves of veterans from the War of 1812 up through the Vietnam War.

OLD GERMAN CHURCH
AND CEMETERY

A Monument to Disappointment

WALDOBORO

Public cemetery

*On Route 32, south of Route 1; the cemetery
is 0.5 mile down on the right on a hill.
Grounds open dawn to dusk.*

The Old German Cemetery is located in the town of Waldoboro, which was settled by German immigrants in 1748. But this little cemetery has three unique stones that don't mark a body beneath the earth; instead, they serve as pronouncements of a sort.

Though services have not been held at the church in more than a century, the building is still well loved by residents in Waldoboro, where it's treated as a traditional northern New England historic site and open for a few hours on weekend afternoons only during July and August. It is one of the oldest churches in Maine, but at first glance you may not know it's a house of worship—it has no steeple.

In any case, the adjacent cemetery is open year-round, and the painstaking attention that was paid to the inscriptions on its tombstones is evident. The most famous stone doesn't mark a grave but is a pronouncement from original settlers, who didn't sound too pleased about ending up in this Down East town. In fact, it almost sounds as if they thought they were tricked into moving to Waldoboro:

THIS TOWN WAS SETTLED IN 1718 BY GERMANS
WHO EMIGRATED TO THIS PLACE WITH THE PROMISE

One of the oldest churches in Maine
(don't be fooled by the lack of a steeple)

AND EXPECTATION OF FINDING A POPULOUS CITY,
INSTEAD OF WHICH THEY FOUND NOTHING BUT A WILDERNESS.
FOR THE FIRST FEW YEARS THEY SUFFERED
TO A GREAT EXTENT BY INDIAN WARS AND STARVATION.

Another stone, for a Civil War soldier from the town named Lowell Brock, also doesn't mark a grave. Instead it reads,

HE WAS TAKEN PRISONER BY THE REBELS, AT FAIR PLAY MD, JULY 10 1863. NO
TIDINGS HAVE BEEN RECEIVED OF HIM SINCE.

And another for Elizabeth M. Castner, the wife of Captain Silas N. Castner. It notes, in part, that she

DIED AT SEA ON BOARD BRIG PEERLESS APRIL 4, 1853, AND WAS BURIED
IN LAT. 27 29' N. LONG. 74 50' W. WHILE ON HER PASSAGE
FROM BOSTON TO HAVANA AE. 27 YRS 4 MOS.

FORT HILL CEMETERY

Food for Worms

WINSLOW

Public cemetery

Route 100A (Halifax Street).
Grounds open dawn to dusk.

Fort Hill Cemetery is the oldest burial ground in Winslow, a small town just east of Waterville. Like most small New England villages, it had—indeed, still has—its fair share of eccentrics.

This becomes crystal clear when you read the unusually lengthy epitaph for former resident Richard Thomas:

> HERE LIES THE BODY OF RICHARD THOMAS
> AN INGLISHMAN BY BIRTH,
> A WHIG OF 76,
> BY OCCUPATION A COOPER,
> NOW FOOD FOR WORMS.
> LIKE AN OLD RUM PUNCHEON MARKED, NUMBERED AND SHOOKED,
> HE WILL BE RAISED AGAIN AND FINISHED BY HIS CREATOR.
> HE DIED SEPT. 28, 1824, AGED 75,
> AMERICA MY ADOPTED COUNTRY,
> MY BEST ADVICE TO YOU IS THIS
> TAKE CARE OF YOUR LIBERTIES.

Mister Thomas left very specific instructions not only about his inscription but also how he wanted his tombstone to appear. Although most stones are polished smooth to prepare for placement in a cemetery, Thomas dictated that while one side of his could be polished, the other had to remain rough-hewn and jagged, the same way it arrived from the quarry.

North South East West

IN A CHRISTIAN GRAVEYARD, BODIES ARE BURIED WITH THE HEAD TO THE WEST AND THE FEET TO THE EAST BUT THE BASIC DIVISION HAS ALWAYS BEEN BETWEEN NORTH AND SOUTH. THE LEFT-HAND SIDE OF THE ALTAR (NORTH) WAS CALLED THE GOSPEL SIDE FOR SINNERS, THE RIGHT-HAND (SOUTH) WAS THE EPISTLE SIDE FOR THE RIGHTEOUS. SO THE UNCLEAN DEAD WERE BURIED TO THE NORTH OF THE GRAVEYARD.

—Nigel Barley, *Grave Matters*

ANCIENT CEMETERY

A Gold Ring & a Fish

WISCASSET

Public cemetery

*Route 218 (Federal Street), just north of
Lincoln Street and north of Route 1.
Grounds open dawn to dusk.*

For a small seacoast town with nothing particularly grand to make it stand out from other small seacoast towns, Wiscasset's Ancient Cemetery contains the graves of numerous influential men through the years.

The earliest stone dates from 1739, for a man by the name of Joshua Pool. Nearby is the stone for Moses Carleton; locals tell a story about him that may or may not be true. Carleton made a great fortune from the sea trade, as did most of the other wealthy inhabitants of the town. One day he removed a gold ring from his finger and threw it in a river. It's rumored he said, "I have about as much chance of seeing that ring again as I have of dying a poor man." A few years later he sat down to a fish dinner, and the same ring he'd tossed into the river was inside the fish. And by the time he died, he had lost his entire fortune.

One of the tallest monuments in the cemetery marks the grave of Samuel Sewall, who served as chief justice of the supreme court of the commonwealth, which at the time of his death in 1814 was a landmass that included both Massachusetts and Maine. The unusual thing about his obelisk is that his epitaph is written entirely in Latin.

The stone for John Dennis McCrate is nearby. McCrate served in the Maine legislature as well as the U.S. House of Representatives; he died in 1879. But perhaps the most poignant tombstone inscription in the cemetery appears on the one for Thomas Woodman, "who died on his passage from Damarara to this Port Sept. 14th 1796." Woodman was fifty-two at the time, and even a cursory look at many of the tombstones in cemeteries on the Maine coast reveals that a good percentage of the residents died while far from home. Woodman's epitaph refers to this:

> IN FOREIGN CLIMES, ALAS! RESIGNS HIS BREATH,
> HIS FRIENDS FAR FROM HIM IN THE HOUR OF DEATH.

Reversal of Fortune

AN ECCENTRIC PERSON NAMED RICHARD HULL WAS BURIED ON HORSEBACK UPSIDE DOWN, IN ORDER THAT HE MIGHT HAVE THE ADVANTAGE OF POSITION ON THE DAY OF JUDGMENT, WHEN ACCORDING TO A ONCE POPULAR NOTION, THE WORLD WOULD BE REVERSED.
—Bertram Puckle, *Funeral Customs*

OLD BURYING YARD

A Witch's Grave

YORK

Public cemetery

Route 1A (York Street), next to Jefferds'
Tavern at the corner of Lindsay Road.
Grounds open dawn to dusk.

People who were suspected of being witches or warlocks in early New England did not have it easy in life, and things usually didn't improve much after death.

Such was the case with Mary Nasson, an herbalist in eighteenth-century York, Maine, who, in addition to prescribing medicinal concoctions for her neighbors, was also frequently called upon to perform exorcisms. Most of the townspeople believed her to be a witch outright, and as such not everyone in York thought very highly of her. When she died at the age of twenty-nine in 1774, legend has it that her husband believed some of the less charitable townspeople would attempt to dig up the grave in order to exorcise the demons within her body.

As a result, he constructed an elaborate grave, with a headstone and footstone, both inscribed with her name, and a huge stone slab that was placed directly over where the casket was interred. When questioned by the community, he explained that the multiple stones were to prevent cattle from tearing up the grave, but nobody believed him. Indeed, no other grave in the area—or throughout New England—contains such a massive stone placed directly on the ground over the casket.

Later on, the story was altered to explain that Mary had been hanged for witchcraft, and the rock was set on her grave to prevent her escape. Here's the inscription:

HERE LIEST QUITE FREE FROM LIFES
DISTRESSING CARE,
A LOVING WIFE
A TENDER PARENT DEAR
CUT DOWN IN MIDST OF DAYS
AS YOU MAY SEE
BUT—STOP—MY GRIEF
I SOON SHALL EQUAL BE
WHEN DEATH SHALL STOP MY BREATH
AND END MY TIME
GOD GRANT MY DUST
MAY MINGLE, THEN, WITH THINE.
SACRED TO THE MEMORY OF MRS. MARY NASSON, WIFE OF MR. SAMUEL
NASSON, WHO DEPARTED THIS LIFE AUG. 18TH 1774, AE 29.

In time, Mary Nasson's grave became known as the Witch's Grave and is probably the most visited stone in the cemetery. In fact, some people believe that the large rock slab radiates heat due to Mary's notorious past. If you go, place your hands on the rock and compare its temperature to that of the headstone and footstone.

MASSACHUSETTS

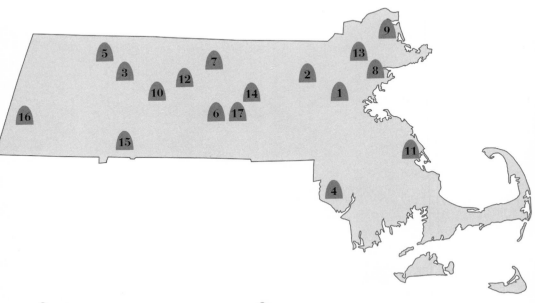

1 Cambridge: Mount Auburn Cemetery

2 Concord: Sleepy Hollow Cemetery

3 Deerfield: Deerfield Cemetery

4 Fall River: Oak Grove Cemetery

5 Greenfield: Green River Cemetery

6 Leicester: Spider Gates Cemetery/
Old Quaker Cemetery

7 Leominster: Evergreen Cemetery

8 Marblehead: Old Burial Hill

9 Newburyport: Old Hill Burying Ground

10 Pelham: Knights Cemetery

11 Plymouth: Burial Hill

12 Quabbin: Quabbin Park Cemetery

13 Salem: Burying Point and Witch
Trial Victims Memorial

14 Shrewsbury: Hillside Cemetery

15 Springfield: Bay Path Cemetery

16 Stockbridge: Center Cemetery

17 Worcester: Hope Cemetery

MOUNT AUBURN CEMETERY

America's First Garden Cemetery

CAMBRIDGE

Private cemetery

580 Mount Auburn Street
Grounds open 8:00 A.M.–5:00 p.m. year-round;
until 7:00 P.M. May–September
(617) 547–7105; www.mountauburn.org.
Map, pamphlets, and public programs available.

Mount Auburn Cemetery is a 170-acre "garden" cemetery that was the first of its kind when a Dr. Jacob Bigelow first conceived of the idea in 1825. He and an esteemed landscape architect of the time, Henry A. S. Dearborn, spent the next six years planning the cemetery on a piece of forestland then known as "Stone's Woods." The first tract of seventy-two acres was purchased in 1829 for $6,000, with the first interment proceeding in 1831. In 1847 a 300-square-foot grave site cost $100. The massive Egyptian granite gate at the entrance to the cemetery was patterned after portals in ancient Greece and cost $10,000 when erected. The cornice, which measures 24 by 12 feet, is a single stone; it was a considerable engineering feat at the time to hoist it up on top of the posts.

Mount Auburn will always serve as a paragon of the kind of cemetery that encourages people to linger due to its sheer beauty, especially when compared to the small, cramped, stony churchyards and town cemeteries that were, even at that time, becoming increasingly crowded—sometimes downright unsafe. It was designed with a Victorian sensibility, and the gently rolling landscape, curvy roads and

Mount Auburn, designed as a "garden,"
is a place to linger.

paths, and sculptures reflect this earlier day. Mount Auburn also contains more than 700 different varieties of trees. In fact, Mount Auburn and the cemeteries that followed, including Green-Wood in Brooklyn, New York, were the precursors of the urban public parks that began to appear a few decades later. It's safe to say that more than half the visitors to the cemetery on any one day then and now don't have a loved one to visit. Bird-watchers also frequent the cemetery in spring and fall, since Mount Auburn is a stopover point for birds of all stripes heading north or south for the season. The common loon, osprey, and snowy owl are just a few of the species viewed here each year.

With the gothic, towering statuary and sculpture and meticulously kept ponds and grounds of Mount Auburn, the buzz of nearby traffic fades into the background as visitors wander through Harvard Hill, Consecration Dell, and Forest Pond.

As of 2003 more than 93,000 people were buried in Mount Auburn, including such distinguished names as Oliver Wendell Holmes, Buckminster Fuller, Julia Ward Howe, Mary Baker Eddy, and Charles Sumner. To fully appreciate the wealth of history and beauty that Mount Auburn represents, rent an audiotape at the entrance to take a self-guided tour through the grounds.

An Early Promotion for Mount Auburn Cemetery

READER! IF YOU WOULD HAVE THE SYMPATHIES OF YOUR NATURE AWAKENED, YOUR EARTHLY AFFECTIONS PURIFIED, YOUR ANXIETIES CHASTENED AND SUBDUED, GO TO MOUNT AUBURN! GO NOT FOR THE GRATIFICATION OF IDLE CURIOSITY . . . GO NOT THERE WITH COLD INDIFFERENCE TO SHOCK THE SENSIBILITY OF THE BEREAVED WITH YOUR ANTIC AND UNSEEMLY BEHAVIOR. . . . BUT GO TO READ AND TO LEARN THE LESSON WHICH YOU MUST TRANSMIT TO THOSE WHO COME AFTER YOU.

—Joseph Buckingham, *Boston Courier*, 1838

SLEEPY HOLLOW CEMETERY

Home of Authors' Ridge

CONCORD

Public cemetery

Route 62 (Bedford Street), off Monument Square.
Grounds open dawn to dusk. (978) 318-3220.

Sleepy Hollow is perhaps one of the most famous cemeteries in Massachusetts, judging by the number of tourists who make the pilgrimage here each year.

The reason is a section of the burial grounds known as "Authors' Ridge," which is well indicated by the many signs throughout the cemetery. Renowned authors of the mid-nineteenth century who called Concord home include Ralph Waldo Emerson, Henry David Thoreau, Louisa May Alcott, and Nathaniel Hawthorne. They lived here, wrote here, walked through the grounds of the cemetery, and are all buried relatively close to one another.

Despite the accomplishments these four writers had in life, their stones bear only their names, with no epitaphs and no ornamentation. Perhaps they wanted the words they wrote in life to speak for them in death. Their stones are simple in design, too: Each is a small slab with the author's full name, except for Emerson's, which is represented by an uncut boulder of granite along with a small bronze sign that bears his name and a brief epitaph.

Often overshadowed by Authors' Ridge is the tomb of Daniel Chester French, the renowned sculptor who created the statue of

Abraham Lincoln for the memorial in Washington, D.C. You can visit one of French's other works by traveling a short distance to the Battleground in Concord to view his statue of the Minuteman.

Daniel Chester French's tomb

DEERFIELD CEMETERY

Burial Site for the Deerfield Massacre

DEERFIELD

Public cemetery

Albany Road, near Deerfield Academy. From Route 10 (Greenfield Road), turn west onto Wells Street, then north onto Main Street. Albany Road is two blocks north. Grounds open dawn to dusk.

Step into Deerfield and it almost seems as though you've left the twenty-first century behind. Indeed, stroll down the main street past Deerfield Academy, past the seventeenth- and eighteenth-century houses, and it may seem like you've instantly left at least a couple of centuries behind—as long as you ignore the cars, that is.

Sometimes it's easy to get caught up in the sheer beauty and artistry of an old New England cemetery: The trees, the stones, the paths—they all seem to be placed just right. Nothing is out of place. You feel like you're back in Victorian times, when Sunday picnics were a regular occasion.

Then you head for the southeast corner of the yard, and you're suddenly reminded what cemeteries are used for: to bury dead bodies. For here is the mass grave of the 1704 Deerfield Massacre victims. A Native American raid—a frequent occurrence at the time—was conducted on the little settlement in Deerfield, which at the time was the westernmost colonial settlement. At least forty-eight villagers were killed and buried in several mounds in the southeast corner of the graveyard; others were kidnapped and forced to march north into Canada.

The detail on this stone depicts Mary, "wife of Simeon Harvey," going to the grave with her infant.

The fifty-seven colonists who survived the 300-plus-mile trek north were held by their captors—Indians and French who both resented the intrusion of the English into what they considered to be their land—for two years until the governor of Massachusetts paid a ransom and sent a ship to carry the captives back to Massachusetts.

OAK GROVE CEMETERY

Burial Site of Lizzie Borden

FALL RIVER

Public cemetery

From Route 6, take Garden Street and head
5 blocks south into the cemetery.
Grounds open dawn to dusk.

I'm not sure if small children are still taught the old rhyme "Lizzie Borden took an ax," but by all accounts the story of the daughter who in 1892 allegedly killed her father and stepmother in Fall River, Massachusetts, still intrigues people today.

Oak Grove is a relatively large cemetery that dates from the nineteenth century, with all the Victorian splendor that implies: elaborate statuary, a gently rolling landscape, and meticulously maintained trees and flowers. Most curious to visitors is that many of the more ornate and highly crafted mortuary sculptures mark the graves of the members of the Borden family, which was quite large. These statues include the figure of a woman draped in lifelike Greek finery and a detailed statue of a man on top of a marble obelisk.

By contrast, the stones for Lizzie—who died in 1927 at the age of sixty-six and was known as Lizbeth—and her parents are very simple, marked with A.J.B. for Andrew, her father, and A.D.B. for Abby, her stepmother. Though Lizzie was acquitted of the murders by a jury, her guilt or innocence has never been proven, and an exhumation and examination of court records by a pathologist were inconclusive.

In her will, Lizzie left $500 to the city of Fall River to pay for perpetual care for her father's grave. The omission of a mention of her stepmother is telling; however, since the family stones are so close together, the city maintains the family plot as a whole, including Lizzie's grave.

Pease Porridge Cold

UNDER THE SOD
UNDER THE TREES
LIES THE BODY OF JONATHAN PEASE
HE IS NOT HERE
BUT ONLY HIS POD
HE HAS SHELLED OUT HIS PEAS
AND GONE TO HIS GOD.
—Epitaph in Old North Cemetery,
Nantucket, Massachusetts

GREEN RIVER CEMETERY
Greenfield's Garden Cemetery

GREENFIELD

Public cemetery

*From Route 2A, head south on River Street
for about 1 mile. Turn right onto Wisdom Way;
the cemetery is on your left. Grounds open
dawn to dusk.*

Yet another cemetery that got its start after the magnificent success of the garden cemetery Mount Auburn in Cambridge is Green River Cemetery, which was established in 1851. The people of Greenfield were so excited that the cemetery would be located in their western Massachusetts town that the dedication ceremony featured a band along with a special hymn to honor the graveyard written by Frederick Goddard Tuckerman, a poet who lived in Greenfield. Here are the first and last verses:

> Beside the River's dark green flow,
> Here, where the pine trees weep,
> Red Autumn's winds will coldly blow
> Above their dreamless sleep:
> . . . .
> So let them lie, their graves bedecked,
> Whose bones these shades invest,
> Nor grief deny, nor fear suspect,
> The beauty of their rest.

The special attraction of a garden cemetery was that not only was it a place to bury loved ones, but the design was intended to mirror facets of life. For instance, the entrance usually rises gently, to symbolize a deliberate transition from the world of the living into the world of the dead. The roads and footpaths through a garden cemetery often move in a circular fashion such that visitors occasionally lose their bearings, as in life. And the garden landscapes and trees reflect the constant change in seasons—again, reminding people that the same thing happens in everyday life, and they should be prepared for the inevitable end.

Of course, most people do not specifically think of these notions while strolling through the cemetery, but it's believable that somehow they do register in the subconscious in the midst of the magnificent beauty of the architecture and stones.

SPIDER GATES CEMETERY/ OLD QUAKER CEMETERY

Ghosts Roam Here

LEICESTER

Private cemetery

Somewhere between Reservoir Drive (Manville Street) and Mulberry Street. Grounds open dawn to dusk.

Spider Gates Cemetery is notorious for being among the most haunted cemeteries in Massachusetts. Unlike most of the old New England graveyards that are purported to be teeming with ghosts, however, this one is actually still used for new burials.

Spider Gates gets its name from—you guessed it—the wrought-iron gates at the entrance that look like spiderwebs, although its official name is Old Quaker Cemetery, or the Friends Cemetery. In any case, it is owned by the Worcester–Pleasant Street Friends in Leicester, and the first burials took place in the eighteenth century; indeed, members of the group are still buried in the cemetery. Locals like to be somewhat vague when giving out directions to ghost hunters who are not from the area. Rumor has it that the locals also ratcheted up the stories about the haunted graveyard by warning strangers that ghosts fly up from the ground in broad daylight, while a rusted car will suddenly appear and seem to head straight for visitors.

In any case, what *is* easy to find in Spider Gates Cemetery is the Hanging Tree, where a local teenager supposedly hung himself in the

1980s. Just look for the rope in the tree, even though it is not the original one; it has been taken and replaced many times over throughout the years.

If you do decide to visit Spider Gates, you should know what others have reported from previous visits: peculiar noises and screams out of nowhere in the middle of the day, cold spots—a phenomenon frequently associated with a ghost passing by—and unexplained smoky, cloudlike images seen in photographs taken at the site.

Preventive Measures

TO PLACE THE CORPSE FACE DOWNWARDS HAS A SPECIAL SIGNIFICANCE. AN OLD SUPERSTITION HAS IT THAT AN INFANT BURIED IN THIS MANNER—IF A FIRST-BORN CHILD—WILL PREVENT ANY FURTHER ADDITIONS TO THE FAMILY. THIS MODE OF BURIAL WAS ALSO HELD TO BE A MEANS OF PREVENTING TROUBLE FROM A WITCH AFTER DEATH.

—Bertram Puckle, *Funeral Customs*

EVERGREEN CEMETERY

Persecuted for Wearing the Beard

LEOMINSTER

Public cemetery

From Route 2, head southwest on Main Street; the cemetery is on your left. Grounds open dawn to dusk.

Some cemeteries you visit for the sheer beauty of the stones and the grounds, while you go to others for the people buried there who hold great places in history. Still others are worth a trip for the tragedies that brought the people buried there to their final rest.

And then there are the cemeteries with one great stone that will make you laugh. Evergreen Cemetery in Leominster is one of these. Located in the front row of graves nearest to the road is a large stone; the portrait of a man with a tremendous beard is sculpted into the rock. Just below the whiskers in question, the inscription reads, "Persecuted for wearing the beard." This is Joseph Palmer's grave site.

You think we're all a bunch of conformists these days? Take a trip back in time to 1830, when men simply did not walk around with facial hair. One day in that year, local resident Joseph Palmer decided he wanted to grow a beard. The other residents of Leominster saw his gesture as a deliberate affront and teased him, yelled epithets at him, and even ran after him with a straightedge razor and soap in an effort to shave it off themselves.

The town constable was called, and Palmer calmly explained what had happened. The policeman charged Palmer for inciting the locals to

* See 1970's pub. on Hist of Fitchburg

riot and escorted him to the town jail. The bearded one sat in jail for at least several weeks because he wouldn't pay the fine the town had levied upon him for his "offense." Eventually they let him go, and though he continued to wear a beard, he moved to a commune known as Fruitlands and lived there until his death. The fact that he decided to be buried in Leominster with his bearded monument makes you think that even though he had left the town long before, he was determined to be buried in Leominster—in the front row of the cemetery, no less— just so he could have the last word.

– See history – Fitchburg –
Dr. Palmer – dentist.
– Octagonal house (gone) built
on upper Main St – Ⓔ

OLD BURIAL HILL

Marblehead's Ornate Cemetery

MARBLEHEAD

Public cemetery

Take Atlantic Avenue (Route 129) east. Turn right onto Washington Street, then left onto Franklin Street, and make an immediate right onto Orne Street. The cemetery is on your left. Grounds open dawn to dusk. www.oldburialhill.org.

Old Burial Hill is a completely stunning cemetery, one that rivals the garden graveyards of the mid-nineteenth century, even though it predates those burial grounds by two centuries. The Marblehead graveyard was established at the site of Marblehead's first meetinghouse, and it has a view that many in town would kill for, or at least pay a handsome sum for: It looks out onto Old Marblehead as well as the harbor and the Atlantic Ocean.

History is palpable at Old Burial Hill. Records estimate that approximately 600 Revolutionary soldiers are buried here, though few of the graves are marked. At the top of the hill is the Fishermen's Monument, built to honor sixty-five fishermen who were lost in the nineteenth century's version of *The Perfect Storm,* a massive hurricane-strength gale that occurred in the Grand Banks of Newfoundland in 1846. Ten ships from the town were lost and never found. The names of all sixty-five men are inscribed on the obelisk.

Near the Fishermen's Monument are several gravestones noteworthy for their ornate portraiture. The stones of Anna Barnard and the Reverend William Whitwell, who died in the late 1700s, have

Susanna Jayne's headstone

detailed carved images of both of the deceased. Elsewhere on the same hill is the renowned stone of Susanna Jayne, who died in 1776. Death images were commonly used on gravestones during the period, but on Jayne's stone, all of them appear: an hourglass, a skeleton, a snake devouring its tail, crossbones, the whole plethora of carvings. This was unusual for a time when carvers and mourning relatives were usually content with just one.

By the way, if you are unable to visit Old Burial Hill in person, do spend some time at their Web site, www.oldburialhill.org, for a marvelous, detailed virtual tour of the cemetery, with great pictures and descriptions of the people who are buried there.

OLD HILL BURYING GROUND

Home of Lengthy Epitaphs

NEWBURYPORT

Public cemetery

Across from Bartlett Mall off High Street.
Grounds open dawn to dusk.

What is it about old New England that caused citizens who were close-mouthed in life to become absolutely verbose on their tombstones? Or vice versa, when an overly talkative person was stingy with words when it came to his epitaph? The Old Hill Burying Ground in Newburyport contains two stellar examples of the craft: a gravestone that doesn't know when to quit, as well as the polar opposite from a man who couldn't keep his mouth or pen quiet in life.

The wordy epitaph can be found at the top of the hill on the stone of Mary McHard. It sounds like something that might roll out of the computer of a really bad romance novelist these days:

[SHE] WAS IN A STATE OF HEALTH SUDDENLY SUMMONED TO THE SKIES AND SNATCHED FROM THE EAGER EMBRACES OF HER FRIENDS (AND THE THROB-BING HEARTS OF HER DISCONSOLATE FAMILY CONFESSED THEIR FAIREST PROSPECTS OF SUBLUNARY BLISS WERE IN ONE MOMENT DASHED) BY SWAL-LOWING A PEA AT HER OWN TABLE, WHENCE IN A FEW HOURS SHE SWEETLY BREATHED HER SOUL AWAY INTO HER SAVIOUR'S ARMS, ON THE 18TH DAY OF MARCH A.D. 1780.

In the next example, while his stone is relatively mundane, the life of "Lord" Timothy Dexter was anything but; his title was conferred on

A reminder of the Revolutionary period

him by locals as a joke, and he took them seriously. Dexter became wealthy by practicing a version of what we now know as buy low–sell high. After he built his fortune, he built himself a mansion and displayed numerous statues of famous people on the grounds, among them Napoleon and Adam and Eve. He also included one of himself with a plaque that read, "I am the first in the East, the first in the West, and

Going in Circles

IN IRELAND IF A FUNERAL PROCESSION PASSES A CHURCH ON THE WAY TO THE CEMETERY, THE MOURNERS MUST CIRCLE THE CHURCH NO FEWER THAN THREE TIMES BEFORE PROCEEDING TO THE GRAVEYARD, OR ELSE THE CORPSE AND PALLBEARERS WILL BE CURSED.

the greatest philosopher in the Western world." He had a predilection for writing books and pamphlets with an overabundance of run-on sentences. He thought readers would be so grateful for the words that spilled from his brain that they would overlook the massive misspellings and grammatical errors. He was wrong. They complained in droves.

He answered their complaints in what he considered to be his masterpiece: *A Pickle for the Knowing Ones,* which he published in 1802. The book was essentially one long, pessimistic ramble about what he thought about everything from religion to the current day. In successive editions, he added two pages that contained only rows of punctuation marks, in response to those who had complained about the lack of commas and periods in earlier volumes. His stone reads:

HE GAVE LIBERAL DONATIONS
IN THE SUPPORT OF THE GOSPEL
FOR THE BENEFIT OF THE POOR
AND FOR OTHER BENEVOLENT PURPOSES.

KNIGHTS CEMETERY

The Arsenic Stone

PELHAM

Public cemetery

From Route 9, take Route 202 north for about 5 miles, then head left onto Packardville Road. Grounds open dawn to dusk.

Just as some towns are known by their industry—some build a reputation on their fabric mills, while others are shoe-factory towns—so some cemeteries attract people from far and wide because of the uniqueness of one particular stone. Knights Cemetery in Pelham has built its reputation on what has come to be known as the "arsenic stone."

Knights is a relatively unobtrusive graveyard with nothing to mark it as being particularly unusual except for a plain stone in the northwest corner of the burial yard. Erected for Warren Gibbs, who died at the age of thirty-six years, five months, and twenty-three days, it contains the following verse:

THINK MY FRIENDS WHEN THIS YOU SEE
HOW MY WIFE HATH DEALT BY ME
SHE IN SOME OYSTERS DID PREPARE
SOME POISON FOR MY LOT AND SHARE;

WHEN OF THE SAME I DID PARTAKE
AND NATURE YIELDED TO ITS FATE
BEFORE SHE MY WIFE BECAME
MARY FELTON WAS HER NAME.
ERECTED BY HIS BROTHER WM. GIBBS

According to local sources, the stone that presently adorns the grave site of Warren Gibbs is at least the third or fourth reproduction. The original stone was stolen, found, and then mysteriously disappeared, supposedly taken by a friend of Warren's widow. It was replaced by a reproduction, which was again stolen in 1940. It was found buried in a resident's basement seven years later, and the Pelham Historical Society took custody of the stone. They then replaced the duplicate with a triplicate and may well have to replace it again in the future.

BURIAL HILL

*Final Resting Place of the
Mayflower Passengers*

PLYMOUTH

Public cemetery

*West of Route 3A in the town center, behind the
First Church. Grounds open dawn to dusk.*

Though nearby Duxbury has a Mayflower Cemetery, Burial Hill in Plymouth is where many of the *Mayflower* passengers are buried. The first interment at Burial Hill took place in 1622; the first fifty *Mayflower* passengers who died during the first winter of 1621 were buried on a smaller hill across from Plymouth Rock. Once the original settlers began to fan out to settle what would later become the outlying towns, and a steady stream of new settlers started to arrive in the New World, they were usually buried in graveyards in the new settlements.

The graveyard was called Fort Hill until 1698, because the Pilgrims had built their first fort in this location in 1622. A long, steep stone staircase leads from the street to the cemetery; the site is said to offer the best view from a cemetery in all of New England, overlooking Plymouth and Cape Cod Bay.

Burial Hill contains numerous early luminaries, including Mary Allerton Cushman, the oldest *Mayflower* passenger at the age of eighty-three, buried here in 1699. There's a monument to Governor William Bradford, who served as governor of Plymouth Colony for thirty years,

Burial Hill overlooks Plymouth and Cape Cod Bay.

winning reelection each year due to his popularity and competence in the face of great hardship. The monument reads:

UNDER THIS STONE REST THE ASHES OF WILLIAM BRADFORD
A ZEALOUS PURITAN AND SINCERE CHRISTIAN
GOV OF PLY. COL. FROM APRIL 1621 TO 1657
(THE YEAR HE DIED AGED 69)
EXCEPT 5 YRS. WHICH HE DECLINED

QUABBIN PARK CEMETERY

Burial Site of Lost Towns

QUABBIN

Public cemetery

*From the center of Ware, follow Route 9
west for about 6 miles. The cemetery is on your
left just before Monson Turnpike Road. Grounds
open dawn to dusk.*

In the early 1900s, Boston needed more water. The most workable option city planners could come up with was to create a reservoir in the central part of the state and then pipe the water into the city.

The only problem was that no natural aquifer or valley existed. They had to create one by flooding a cluster of valley towns large enough to hold sufficient water for the entire city.

It took the public works department and Boston officials nearly four decades to come up with a feasible plan. By 1939 the towns that made up the valley—Dana, Enfield, Greenwich, and Prescott—were condemned and declared unfit for habitation; residents had no choice but to accept the modest buyout offer. But what to do about the thirty-four cemeteries and almost 8,000 grave sites that remained behind? Planners decided to build a new cemetery near the reservoir.

Ground for the eighty-two-acre Quabbin Park Cemetery was broken in 1931, years before the area was to be abandoned and subsequently flooded. The remains from the thirty-four cemeteries in the towns that were to be obliterated—or located on land earmarked for a watershed surrounding the new reservoir—were exhumed and reinterred in the new cemetery. In all, 7,613 graves were relocated, with just over 1,000 going to other cemeteries in the area.

Contrary to popular belief all of the known and identified grave sites were relocated. The burial sites for various Native American tribes that had previously lived in the area are now underwater, since these tribal burial yards had few markers, as was their custom. In addition the aggressive settlement efforts of the colonists and their ancestors meant that development usually occurred right over the sites without their knowledge.

Today Quabbin Reservoir covers 39 square miles and is 18 miles long, with an average depth of 51 feet; it holds 412 billion gallons of water. The reservoir serves as a wildlife sanctuary and popular hiking area on the 40,000 acres set aside for recreational use.

BURYING POINT AND WITCH TRIAL VICTIMS MEMORIAL

The Crucible

SALEM

Public cemetery

51 Charter Street, 1 block north of Derby Street.
Grounds open dawn to dusk.

Salem's Burying Point and Witch Trial Victims Memorial represent at once the best and worst of early colonial history. While the graves of Simon Bradstreet, an early governor of Massachusetts, and Roger More, one of the original *Mayflower* Pilgrims, are here, the graveyard is also home to a memorial for the twenty victims who were accused of practicing witchcraft during the famous Salem trials and subsequently sentenced to death.

Judge John Hathorne, the chief judge who presided over the Salem Witch Trials of 1692, is buried here. His great-great-grandson was Nathaniel Hawthorne. It's rumored that Nathaniel added a *w* to his name in order to distance himself from his not-so-savory ancestor. Grimshawe House, where Nathaniel's wife lived after he died, is just adjacent to the cemetery.

Though the witch trial memorial is adjacent to the Burying Point cemetery, you have to walk through the cemetery to reach the memorial section. No one knows where the "witches" were actually buried; they were not allowed to be interred in consecrated ground because they were believed to be "of the Devil." Each of the twenty stones contains the name of the victim, the method of death, and the date of death.

In order to preserve ancient stones that have
become brittle through the years, preservation societies
frequently encase them in concrete.

Usually the families of the hanged claimed the bodies and buried them on private land.

To get more of a taste of what life was like back then, head over to the Witch Museum to see the Dungeon, a re-creation of the prison where the accused "witches" were held. The tiny stone cells had no light or heat; to further add insult to injury, the prisoners had to pay for not only their room and board but also the expense of their own hanging.

As can be expected, Halloween in Salem is a bit like Mardi Gras in New

The gravestone of Mrs. Isabella Wildrage, who died in 1780.

Orleans: crowded. Well over 100,000 people come from all over the world to celebrate the holiday in the town, so according to your own temperament, you may want to head there for the festivities or visit during a calmer time of year.

HILLSIDE CEMETERY

Graveyard for Worcester State Hospital

SHREWSBURY

Public cemetery

214 Lake Street. From Route 9, head south on Lake Street for about 0.5 mile. The cemetery is on the grounds of the Glavin Regional Center on the right. Grounds open dawn to dusk.

There are undoubtedly thousands of abandoned old family cemeteries throughout New England today that don't appear on current maps. Another kind of abandoned cemetery that few consider—or even realize exist—are the final resting places for the patients who had been longtime residents at hospitals or psychiatric homes, back in the days when mental illness was not mentioned in polite company.

The Worcester State Hospital in Shrewsbury operated Hillside Farm as a home for its permanent residents. When a patient died, a relative would sometimes claim the body for burial in a family cemetery, but more often interment took place in the Hillside Cemetery on the farm. More than 1,600 patients were buried here between 1918 and 1989, when the hospital was shut down. Each grave site was marked only with a brick that had a number written on it.

After the hospital closed, to be replaced by a state-run regional mental health center, the cemetery quickly took on the look of one that had been abandoned some time ago; it went unmaintained for years and became overgrown with weeds. Finally, however, staffers at the center took it upon themselves to clean up the cemetery and—more important—to replace the numbered brick grave markers with proper flat stones listing the name of the deceased as well as the dates of birth and death. Checking and cross-referencing records kept at the city clerk's office with death certificates from the old hospital, they spent a couple of years researching the history of the former residents. Today the cemetery is a place where the buried are remembered with dignity.

Peace Is Cheap

SACRED TO THE MEMORY OF ANTHONY DRAKE,
WHO DIED FOR PEACE AND QUIETNESS SAKE;
HIS WIFE WAS CONSTANTLY SCOLDING AND SCOFFIN',
SO HE SOUGHT FOR REPOSE IN A TWELVE-DOLLAR COFFIN.
—Epitaph in Burlington, Massachusetts

BAY PATH CEMETERY

Springfield's Poorhouse Graveyard

SPRINGFIELD

Public cemetery

Blunt Park, off Roosevelt Avenue.
Grounds open dawn to dusk.

Just as the Worcester State Hospital had a cemetery for its patients, Springfield needed a graveyard for the town's poorhouse, which was built in 1873 and operated through 1952. The Bay Path Cemetery served as the burial yard for what was once the almshouse, or poorhouse, for the city. Keeping with its other commonly known name, a poor farm, this almshouse was actually located on a farm, in then-rural Springfield.

According to local taphophile Roberta Cyr, who has researched the burial grounds for the poorhouse, more than 1,000 burials took place at the yard. No names appeared on the grave markers. Instead, numbers were used to refer to a specific resident, whose name was referenced in a hand-copied booklet available at the Connecticut Valley Historical Museum, except for infants, who were ordinarily listed only as "Infant" in city records.

As part of the Works Progress Administration's public works projects during the Depression, local men were hired to neaten up the cemetery by digging up graves and arranging them in rows. In the years since the poor farm closed, maintenance has been spotty. Though the Springfield Historical Society cleaned the site in 1981, the graveyard had become so overgrown that it was difficult to tell it was a cemetery.

Today it's cleaned up once more, with a sign hanging on the front fence to identify it.

CENTER CEMETERY

Grave Site of Norman Rockwell

STOCKBRIDGE

Public cemetery

At the corner of Main and Church Streets.
Grounds open dawn to dusk

Although most visitors come to Center Cemetery in Stockbridge to view the grave of Norman Rockwell, who died in 1978, if they stumble around the old cemetery a bit, they'll find a wonderful array of quirky, unusual stones and even a family plot that shows that those with an iron fist can still choose to rule from beyond the grave.

Rockwell's stone is pretty simple, with just his last name to mark it. After viewing it, head toward the back of the cemetery to the Sedgwick family plot. Theodore Sedgwick was a prominent lawyer who helped to free a slave named Elizabeth Freeman in a Massachusetts courtroom in 1783. Afterward, she worked for the Sedgwick family, and her stone is included in the Sedgwick plot. Theodore went on to become both a congressman and a senator.

But that's not the most unusual thing about it. Theodore—the great-great-great-grandfather of Edie, the noted 1960s devotee of Andy Warhol—designed the burial plot himself, with his stone in the middle, and all family descendants buried around him in concentric circles that resemble a gigantic pie. Old Theodore did this because he believed that when Judgment Day arrived and all his relatives rose from the dead, the first thing his relations would see would be him. By the way, Edie, who died of a drug overdose, is here, too.

The epitaph for Elizabeth Freeman—known as Mum Bet—was written by Theodore's daughter, Catharine Maria Sedgwick, the author of several novels, who died in 1867. One of her most controversial works was a book titled *Married or Single,* which she wrote to justify her very unusual choice to remain unmarried.

Here's the epitaph:

> HER SUPPOSED AGE WAS 85 YEARS.
> SHE WAS BORN A SLAVE AND
> REMAINED A SLAVE FOR NEARLY THIRTY YEARS.
> SHE COULD NEITHER READ NOR WRITE YET IN
> HER OWN SPHERE SHE HAD NO
> SUPERIOR NOR EQUAL. SHE NEITHER
> WASTED TIME NOR PROPERTY.
> SHE NEVER VIOLATED A TRUST NOR FAILED TO PERFORM A DUTY.
> IN EVERY SITUATION OF DOMESTIC
> TRIAL SHE WAS THE MOST EFFICIENT
> HELPER, AND THE TENDEREST FRIEND.
> GOOD MOTHER, FAREWELL.

HOPE CEMETERY

Worcester's Garden Cemetery

WORCESTER

Public cemetery

119 Webster Street. Grounds open dawn to dusk.
www.friendsofhopecemetery.com.

Determined not to be eclipsed—as usual—by big-city doings farther east, Worcester decided to start its own garden cemetery in 1852, a few short years after Mount Auburn was founded in Cambridge. Beginning at 50 acres, Hope Cemetery grew over the years to its current area of 168 acres. Today it's listed on the National Register of Historic Places and provides a coherent picture of the history of Worcester and its people through the years.

And those people cover a vast spectrum of accomplishment and society. At the Coes lot, marked by the statue of a grieving angel, Loring Coes is buried, one of the inventors of the monkey wrench. The poet Elizabeth Bishop was born in Worcester, and though she left the city early in life, her family has a plot in Hope Cemetery; an inscription to honor her achievements was added to the Bishop monument in 1997.

There's a handsome Firemen's Monument that was erected and dedicated in 1896; the model for the sculpture was Simon E. Coombs, who was chief of the Worcester Fire Department from 1872 until 1891. A monument to honor Peter Slater, the youngest participant in the Boston Tea Party, was erected in his memory in 1870, as he spent most of his adult life in Worcester. For its time, Hope Cemetery was remarkably diverse, in a nation where particular ethnic groups and races were

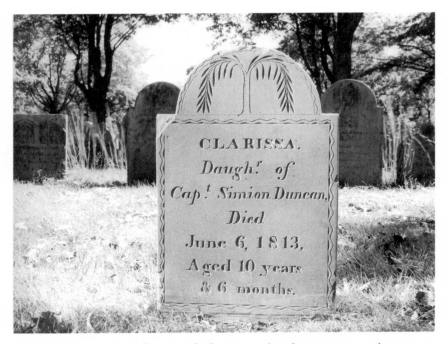

CLARISSA.
Daugh.ʳ of.
Cap.ᵗ Simion Duncan,
Died
June 6, 1813,
Aged 10 years
& 6 months.

The weeping willow symbolizes grief and mourning, in this case for the loss of a 10-year-old girl.

barred from burial in a large number of cemeteries. The First Jewish Burial Grounds at Hope Cemetery was instituted in 1881, and together there are seven Jewish sections throughout the cemetery. A Norwegian Plot also exists in the graveyard.

A surprisingly large number of mausoleums also dot the landscape, including the Norcross Mausoleum, an impressive structure built in 1903 that imitates an open Roman Doric temple. Its elaborate detail is no surprise, however; the Norcross family ran one of the best-known architecture firms in the country in the late nineteenth century. In addition to the mausoleum, Norcross projects included the New York Public Library and the remodeling of the current White House.

New Hampshire

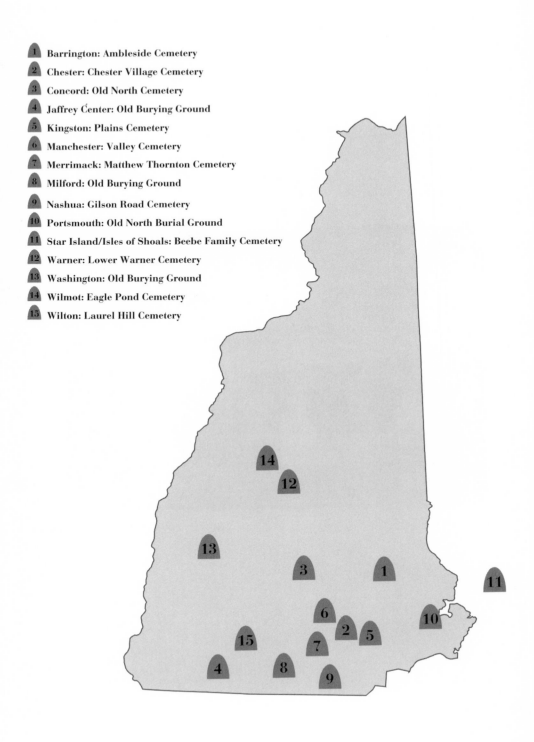

1 Barrington: Ambleside Cemetery

2 Chester: Chester Village Cemetery

3 Concord: Old North Cemetery

4 Jaffrey Center: Old Burying Ground

5 Kingston: Plains Cemetery

6 Manchester: Valley Cemetery

7 Merrimack: Matthew Thornton Cemetery

8 Milford: Old Burying Ground

9 Nashua: Gilson Road Cemetery

10 Portsmouth: Old North Burial Ground

11 Star Island/Isles of Shoals: Beebe Family Cemetery

12 Warner: Lower Warner Cemetery

13 Washington: Old Burying Ground

14 Wilmot: Eagle Pond Cemetery

15 Wilton: Laurel Hill Cemetery

AMBLESIDE CEMETERY
Fender-Bender Central

BARRINGTON

Public cemetery

Route 125 and Lee Oak Road.
Grounds open dawn to dusk.

Ambleside Cemetery has the dubious distinction of being the cemetery in the state of New Hampshire that has caused the most traffic accidents. Founded in the nineteenth century, it adjoins a heavily trafficked crossroads.

In any case, Ambleside Cemetery is a small, well-kept cemetery. Unfortunately, a grove of evergreens envelops the graveyard; the ensuing piles of pine needles can grow to several inches deep around the stones, many of which are thus discolored by this acidic accumulation.

In many respects, it is a typical old cemetery in a small New England town. First situated at a main street in the nineteenth century both for the sake of convenience as well as to serve as a daily reminder to passersby of their own mortality, it did just that for decades. Then development on the busy New Hampshire seacoast area began to spill over to surround Ambleside; Route 125 turned into a major thoroughfare. In more heavily populated areas to the south, some folks wouldn't have thought twice about exhuming the bodies and reinterring them in another, newer cemetery, maybe even one with stones that lay flush with the ground, making for easier groundskeeping and maintenance.

But like most other small-town New England residents, the people who live in Barrington would never think of removing the old graveyard. Indeed, some residents who have gotten into a fender bender in front of the cemetery wear a dent in the door of their truck as a badge of honor.

CHESTER VILLAGE CEMETERY
The Mystery of the Frowning Faces

CHESTER

Public cemetery

The south side of Route 102, just east of Route 121.
Grounds open dawn to dusk.

The Chester Village Cemetery is one of the oldest in the state and was listed on the National Register of Historic Places in 1979. A variety of noted New Hampshirites are buried here, including numerous veterans from the Revolutionary War and two former governors of the Granite State. A clockmaker famous in the eighteenth century, Isaac Blaisdell, also rests here. While visitors glance at their stones with the proper amount of muted respect, that's not the reason why people from all over flock to this cemetery.

It's the faces. Specifically, the frowns on the faces carved on the early tombstones. Seems that while the faces of angels and other heavenly beings made regular appearances on cemetery tombstones in eighteenth- and nineteenth-century New England, the vast majority wore neither smiles nor frowns, but an emotionless straight line for a mouth.

Not in Chester. Instead, some conspicuously wear big smiles, while others have troublesome frowns. People in Chester offer a number of different explanations for why this is so. One rumor has it that the primary stonecutter—who liked to carve smiling faces—got into a feud with the town government; to retaliate, he began etching frowns instead. Another story has it that the same stonecutter was converted to evangelical Christianity, and after many failed attempts to convert his

Most New England stonecarvers depicted
blank expressions; this was not the
case in Chester.

neighbors, he began to carve frowns on his commissioned stones. And
yet another story says there were actually two stonecutters involved,
brothers named Abel and Stephen Webster, and while they worked,
they essentially placed bets on which of the deceased were going to
heaven and which were headed in the other direction. Heaven-bound
got smiles while, well, you know.

Regardless of conjecture, the firmest research says that Stephen's
faces frown while Abel's smile, but no one can explain the reasons
behind the brothers' differing styles.

OLD NORTH CEMETERY

Burial Spot of
New Hampshire's Only President

CONCORD

Public cemetery

North State Street.
Grounds open dawn to dusk.

Concord, the capital city of New Hampshire, surprises visitors with its sheer accessibility. It's a common sight to see the governor walking down State Street, and legislators of every stripe dine in coffee shops along the main drag and stop to chat on the steps of the statehouse. With 400 representatives and 24 senators, New Hampshire's legislature is one of the largest elected government bodies in the country.

The burial place of New Hampshire's sole president is equally accessible. A short drive up North State Street from the town center is the Old North Cemetery, where many of Concord's first settlers are buried. Also buried here is the only U.S. president to be born in New Hampshire, Franklin Pierce, the fourteenth commander in chief of the United States. History has not looked kindly on Pierce, who served only one term from 1853 to 1857 and was judged to be pretty much incompetent, but if Oprah were to talk with him today, she'd undoubtedly have no trouble ferreting out the reason why.

Franklin and his wife, Jane, had three children, but they all died as youths while the family was still living in New Hampshire. Indeed, the last to die, an eleven-year-old son, perished just months before Pierce's inauguration. Pierce subsequently interpreted these events as an

Fourteenth president Franklin Pierce buried his three
children at Old North Cemetery.

indication from God that he was not up to the job and never should
have run, much less been elected. His performance showed it.

Pierce returned to New Hampshire after his term ended, and he
died in 1869. He is buried in a simple grave in the back of the cemetery;
his stone and those of other family members are enclosed by an iron
enclosure that you can enter via a gate.

OLD BURYING GROUND

New Hampshire's Quintessential Old Cemetery?

JAFFREY CENTER

Public cemetery

Route 124, 2 miles west of Jaffrey.
Grounds open dawn to dusk.

When playwright Thornton Wilder set the third act of his play *Our Town* in a cemetery in Grover's Corner, New Hampshire, some believed he patterned the fictional town after nearby Peterborough. But it could just as easily have been the Old Burying Ground in nearby Jaffrey Center. Indeed, many tourists who pass through this small town in the southwest Monadnock region of the state see the classic graveyard with the classic eighteenth-century architecture looming beside it, and decide to stop for a walk and perhaps a lunch. Many a tour guide writer has referred to the cemetery with that perennially overused word, *quintessential*.

The Old Burying Ground in Jaffrey Center has distinctions all its own, as it's the final resting place of the novelist Willa Cather. Located in the southwest corner of the cemetery, Cather's stone holds an epitaph from what was probably her most famous work, *My Ántonia:*

THAT IS HAPPINESS, TO BE DISSOLVED INTO
SOMETHING COMPLETE AND GREAT.

Another distinguished grave site at the Old Burying Ground

Grave site of novelist Willa Cather

belongs to Amos Fortune, a slave who bought freedom for his wife and himself in the mid-eighteenth century. His stone reads:

TO THE MEMORY OF AMOS FORTUNE, WHO WAS BORN FREE IN AFRICA, HE PURCHASED LIBERTY, PROFESSED CHRISTIANITY, LIVED REPUTABLY, AND DIED HOPEFULLY, NOVEMBER 17, 1801, AGED 91.

The Burying Ground is part of the Jaffrey Center Historic District, which was listed on the National Register of Historic Places in 1975.

PLAINS CEMETERY

*Final Resting Place of
the* Real *Josiah Bartlett*

KINGSTON

Public cemetery

*West of Route 111, on the far side of the Kingston
common, across from the Bartlett House.
Grounds open dawn to dusk.*

Plains Cemetery in Kingston is the burial site of Josiah Bartlett. No, not the modern-day TV version; *this* Josiah Bartlett was born in 1729 and died in 1795. He was the sixth governor of New Hampshire and one of three men from the state who signed the Declaration of Independence. People who live in the Granite State just take it as a given that the creator of the television show *The West Wing* would name the show's president after one of New Hampshire's finest sons.

Josiah Bartlett was a physician who practiced medicine in Kingston for forty-five years. He married his first cousin, Mary, in 1754; together they raised twelve children at their New Hampshire farm. When Josiah spent weeks at a time in Philadelphia at the Continental Congress, helping to hammer out the details of the Declaration of Independence, they frequently wrote letters back and forth. Smallpox was a constant threat both in New Hampshire and in Pennsylvania, and in one letter Josiah advised Mary to hold his correspondence over the smoke from the hearth fire before opening it.

Mary died in 1789, while Josiah expired in 1795. Three of their sons became physicians, and seven of Mary and Josiah's grandsons became doctors as well.

The name Josiah Bartlett first belonged to an eighteenth-century New Hampshire governor.

VALLEY CEMETERY

Manchester's Garden Cemetery

MANCHESTER

Public cemetery

*Take Elm Street south to Valley Street, then turn left
onto Pine Street. The cemetery is on your left.
Grounds open dawn to dusk.
www.valley-cemetery.com.*

Though much mention is made of the large garden cemeteries that had their heyday in the middle of the nineteenth century, such as Cambridge's Mount Auburn, few people realize that smaller New England cities were caught up in the garden cemetery craze as well.

One prime example is Valley Cemetery in Manchester, dedicated in 1841. It was created on twenty acres of land donated by the Amoskeag Manufacturing Company, which at the time had hundreds of employees and therefore a vested interest in having a cemetery nearby. Indeed, there was a real demand for cemetery space, since Manchester was one of the prime manufacturing centers of northern New England due to the massive waterpower provided by the Merrimack River. Numerous mills and other factories sprang up along the river down to the Massachusetts line.

Truly, the decision to create a cemetery was prescient, since most of the burial plots at Valley Cemetery were bought up in less than two decades, which created the need for another municipal cemetery nearby, Pine Grove Cemetery.

Valley Cemetery is a monument to the early history of Manchester and New Hampshire as well: Two governors, several town mayors,

Valley Cemetery is a nineteenth-century garden cemetery.

Revolutionary War veterans, and at least sixty soldiers from the Civil War are buried here.

Unfortunately, perhaps due to the fact that few recent burials have taken place, Valley Cemetery has fallen into disrepair, with graves and stones in need of maintenance; graffiti covers even Governor Frederick Smythe's tomb. Concerned area taphophiles formed the Friends of the Valley Cemetery in 2001 and are working hard to restore the grounds and monuments to their former Victorian garden glory; you can contact them at P.O. Box 1316, Manchester, NH 03105 or visit www.valley-cemetery.com.

An Early Proponent of Garden Cemeteries

SO IMPORTANT DO I CONSIDER CHEERFUL ASSOCIATION WITH DEATH, THAT I WISH TO SEE OUR GRAVEYARDS LAID OUT WITH WALKS AND TREES AND BEAUTIFUL SHRUBS AS PLACE OF PROMENADE.

—Lydia Maria Child, *Advice to Mothers*, 1831

MATTHEW THORNTON CEMETERY

*Grave Site of the Last Signer
of the Declaration of Independence*

MERRIMACK

Public cemetery

*Northbound lane of Route 3 in Thornton's
Ferry, a village within Merrimack.
Grounds open dawn to dusk.*

This cemetery is named after Dr. Matthew Thornton, one of three men from New Hampshire to sign the Declaration of Independence (along with Josiah Bartlett and William Whipple). His signature is the last to appear on the document because he arrived late to the meeting. Initially, the others refused to let him place his John Hancock on the paper, but Thornton was adamant. He said he deserved the "same privilege as the others, to be hanged for my patriotism."

After retiring from public office in 1789, Dr. Thornton moved to Merrimack, where he lived until his death in 1803. Thornton's house, known today as the Signer's House, is directly across the street from the cemetery.

The cemetery itself is well kept, and Thornton's grave lies amid others in an unimpressive fashion, typical for New Hampshire. The inscription on his stone, as well as those surrounding it, is barely legible after two centuries of New Hampshire weather. A memorial for Thornton is adjacent to the cemetery, and there's also a New Hampshire historical marker commemorating the physician just alongside the road separating the cemetery from the house.

The memorial for Dr. Matthew Thornton is more
impressive than his gravestone.

OLD BURYING GROUND
(AKA ELM STREET CEMETERY)

Scathing Final Words

MILFORD

Public cemetery

*Route 101A (Elm Street), near Cottage Street.
Grounds open dawn to dusk.*

Talk about grudges, real or imagined. Even in death, there are those who just simply can't let go and must have the last word by scorning their accusers in an epitaph.

Case in point: the Caroline H. Cutter stone in Milford's Old Burying Ground, which lies in the last row of the cemetery on the east. It contains a 140-word epitaph written and commissioned by Caroline's husband Calvin, a physician, after her death. In essence, he rebuked the local church for accusing his wife of lying. She was never completely able to put their minds at rest, and so her reputation suffered, as did that of Dr. Cutter by extension.

The epitaph reads, in part:

MURDERED BY THE BAPTIST MINISTRY AND BAPTIST CHURCHES AS FOLLOWS:
SEPT. 28, 1838. . . . THE INTENTIONAL AND MALICIOUS DESTRUCTION OF HER
CHARACTER AND HAPPINESS, AS ABOVE DESCRIBED, DESTROYED HER LIFE. HER
LAST WORDS UPON THE SUBJECT WERE "TELL THE TRUTH, AND THE INIQUITY
WILL COME OUT."

The church members must have gotten the point—or Dr. Cutter's paranoia must have ceased—since a plaque for Carrie, Dr. Cutter's nineteen-year-old daughter from his subsequent marriage, was mercifully brief:

SHE WAS THE FIRST FEMALE TO ENTER THE SERVICE OF HER COUNTRY IN THE CIVIL WAR, THE FIRST THAT FELL AT HER POST, AND THE FIRST TO FORM ORGANIZED EFFORTS TO SUPPLY THE SICK OF THE ARMY.

I'll Drink to That

"MY GLASS IS RUM."

ALTHOUGH THIS WAS A STONECUTTER'S MISTAKE—THE CORRECT PHRASE IS MY GLASS IS RUN—IT PROBABLY OFFERS AN ACCURATE APPRAISAL OF THE CAUSE OF THE DEMISE OF JAMES EWINS, LAID TO REST IN FOREST HILL CEMETERY IN EAST DERRY, NEW HAMPSHIRE, IN 1781.

GILSON ROAD CEMETERY

*One of New Hampshire's
Most Haunted Graveyards*

NASHUA

Public cemetery

*Take the Dunstable Road exit (5 W) off Route 3
(Everett Turnpike). Follow Dunstable Road south for
about 2 miles, then turn right onto Gilson Road.
Grounds open dawn to dusk.*

At one time Gilson Road Cemetery was reputed to be one of New Hampshire's most haunted cemeteries. Local history blames the once constant manifestation of ghosts on a number of violent battles among different Native American tribes in the area during the 1600s. Whatever the reason, local ghost hunters have admitted—with much dismay—that paranormal auras have eased up in the last decade, ever since a housing development went in across the street.

The question that naturally arises is that of the-chicken-or-the-egg: If somebody didn't have a clue about the notoriety of Gilson Road Cemetery and just happened to stroll across it one day, whether or not that person tended to be naturally receptive to seeing and feeling paranormal spirits, would ghosts show up? In other words, are you more prone to see ghosts—whether or not you personally believe in them—if the seed has been planted that this is a particularly haunted cemetery?

Adding to the mystique of Gilson Road Cemetery is the fact that almost half the people who were buried here have unmarked graves,

? Paupers - Quakers - ?

according to local cemetery records. Little is known about why they were not honored with even a simple gravestone or marker, and no one seems to know where or when the bodies were buried.

Another little-known bit of information is that the cemetery was once a twenty-eight-acre Superfund site known as the Sylvester hazardous waste dump site. Although cleanup was completed in 1983, maybe this explains the preponderance of ghosts: All those chemicals agitated them for so long that they still run around, albeit exceedingly well preserved.

OLD NORTH BURIAL GROUND
One of Portsmouth's Oldest Cemeteries

PORTSMOUTH

Public cemetery

Maplewood Avenue. Grounds open dawn to dusk.

In 1753 the bustling port city of Portsmouth needed a cemetery. Though it already had several town cemeteries, including Point of Graves Cemetery, which was deeded to the town in 1671, burial space was running out. Colonel John Hart, commander of the New Hampshire Regiment at Louisburg, sold a plot of land on what is now Maplewood Avenue for the cemetery. Given that it was the only town cemetery with adequate burial space during a very important part of the city's and the nation's history, a number of very prominent people are buried here, including many Revolutionary War veterans, former New Hampshire governors, and William Whipple, one of the three signers of the Declaration of the Independence who hailed from New Hampshire.

Perhaps the most noteworthy ceremony to take place in the cemetery occurred back in 1908, when a group of veterans who lived in Portsmouth dedicated a grave marker to a man by the name of Prince Whipple, an African American who served in George Washington's military entourage. Prince Whipple's claim to fame was that his was the only black face to appear in the famous painting *Washington Crossing the Delaware River.* Some historians believe that almost 200 black men from New Hampshire were active participants in the Revolutionary War.

Prince Whipple's started out as a sad story: Born in Africa, his parents sent him by boat to America for schooling, but the captain of the

Gravestones for small children are often a cemetery's most poignant.

boat steered him into a slave auction upon reaching Baltimore. General William Whipple, from Portsmouth, purchased Prince and then freed him during the height of the Revolutionary War. Prince then proceeded to serve as one of Washington's attendants, and the rest is history.

Almost. Though Prince Whipple died in 1796 at the age of thirty-two and was buried in Old North Burial Ground, he did not receive a military commendation until the 1908 ceremony.

Ode to a Workaholic

THE LAND I CLEARED IS NOW MY GRAVE
THINK WELL MY FRIENDS HOW YOU BEHAVE.

—Epitaph for Daniel Emerson, in East Cemetery,
Marlboro, New Hampshire

BEEBE FAMILY CEMETERY

A Tragedy of Two Daughters

STAR ISLAND/ISLES OF SHOALS

Private cemetery

On the grounds of the Oceanic Hotel.
Grounds open dawn to dusk.

The Isles of Shoals is a chain of small islands situated about 8 miles off the coast of Portsmouth. Today only one of the islands is inhabited on a seasonal basis—Star Island, once known as Gosport—but in their heyday, the islands were all inhabited year-round, mostly by a class of rough fishermen from the early days of settlement in the seventeenth century.

Occasionally missionaries would choose to live among the "heathen" fishermen to try to civilize the men, who usually showed no signs of being changed. In 1857 the Reverend George Beebe moved his family to Gosport to try his hand at bringing religion to the island population, which numbered less than one hundred.

Back in the nineteenth century, consumption (we know it as tuberculosis) was a much-feared disease almost everywhere in the United States. Visitors with the disease came to the island to try to recover, while native islanders often died from the affliction as it spread among themselves.

As part of his ministerial duties, the Reverend Beebe helped clear land for a cemetery for the islanders. He also helped erect a monument in the graveyard to Captain John Smith, the explorer who was the first to use the term *New England* to refer to the region. At the time, the reverend would never have guessed that three of his daughters would rest in the only graves in the cemetery. In the summer of 1863, his family fell ill with consumption, and three of his daughters died. Two of their gravestones—for Millie and Mitty—remain, well weathered and lichen-covered. The third is so worn that the inscription is illegible.

Below Millie's name the worn memorial reads:

DYING SHE KNEELED DOWN AND PRAYED: PLEASE JESUS,
TAKE ME UP TO THE LIGHTED PLACE. AND HE DID.

The inscription on her sister Mitty's stone is no less haunting:

I DON'T WANT TO DIE, BUT I'LL DO JUST AS JESUS WANTS ME TO.

The Reverend Beebe and his surviving family members managed to stay on the island after their daughters died, but it's easy to perceive that they lost the heart for the area after the deaths. They ended up moving inland and north to Littleton, New Hampshire, four years later.

LOWER WARNER CEMETERY

A Hidden Cemetery

WARNER

Public cemetery

*Take Exit 8 off Interstate 89 to Route 103 east. Take
your first right onto what looks like a wide shoulder
and a driveway. This is the cemetery entrance.
Grounds open dawn to dusk.*

You've probably heard about cemeteries being moved in order to put in
a road. But have you ever heard of a road being built around a cemetery to avoid moving the stones and bones?

This is what happened with the Lower Warner Cemetery. When
the interstate system was in its infancy and was mapped through New
Hampshire, the planners designed the road to run in a gentle north-
westerly direction, skimming mountain ranges that would have
required a huge amount of dynamite and skirting certain towns where
it was rumored that the higher-ups in New Hampshire's congressional
offices had friends and acquaintances to whom favors were owed.

When they got to Warner, right in the middle of their proposed
roadway lay a small town cemetery, complete with a massive white
marble tomb and more than a few veterans of the Civil War. The citizens were adamant about keeping their cemeteries intact, interstate or
no interstate. Even though the federal government had taken farms,
land, and town property all along the corridor via eminent domain,
planners decided, rather than fight the locals, to design the road around
the cemetery, with the northbound lanes to the east and southbound to
the west.

Lower Warner Cemetery has interstate lanes on both sides.

Today the contrast between the graveyard and the constant rush of traffic to both sides—combined with the predominance of nineteenth-century stones and landscaping—makes for a bit of a weird experience. It almost feels as if the interstate was here first, and the cemetery was plopped down in the middle of it from some nineteenth-century time machine. If you hold your hands over your ears, it's actually quite a peaceful place. Trees have grown up around the perimeter of the cemetery to hide it almost entirely from the road. Indeed, there's no sign to mark the graveyard, and it is technically inactive, with the last burial taking place long before the interstate was a glimmer in some senior bureaucrat's eye.

OLD BURYING GROUND

Final Resting Spot of a Leg

WASHINGTON

Public cemetery

*Take Faxon Hill Road from Route 31 to the
cemetery on the right side of the road.
Grounds open dawn to dusk.*

While poor old Colonel Buck of Bucksport, Maine, had a witch's curse placed on him, causing the image of a woman's leg forever to appear on his tombstone, a grave marker in this small village cemetery has something in common with Colonel Buck: a leg.

But not the curse of a witch's leg. Instead, an actual leg is buried in Washington's Old Burying Ground. You see, Captain Samuel Jones lost a leg in 1804 in an accident, and perhaps to stave off those towns-people who might want to tease him with the then timely nickname of Pegleg, or Pe'leg in some circles, he chose a different path.

Or perhaps the leg had simply served him well, and he wanted to pay it proper respect with a decent burial. In any case, the town turned out for the funeral and subsequent burial of the leg, though no town or church record exists for said burial, so it's impossible to say how elaborate the service was, or if a horse and carriage was hired to transport the leg from church to churchyard. And then, of course, there's the question of the casket—if any—that served as the final resting place of the esteemed leg. Some mysteries will never be solved.

What is known is that the leg was buried in its own plot near the road, distinguished by a slate marker that reads:

CAPT. SAMUEL JONES LEG WHICH WAS AMPUTATED JULY 7, 1804.

It's also known that the grave site has so far served as a real conversation starter, for locals and visitors alike, getting everyone talking about Captain Jones's leg. Perhaps that's all he intended.

Still, a bigger question remains: When Captain Jones finally died, he was buried in Boston. The old colonists used to believe that upon Resurrection Day all the buried would rise up and face their God. They believed that the body had to be intact—with no body parts missing and certainly not cremated—in order to make it to heaven. In Captain Jones's case, will the leg beat feet to Boston first, or will most of Captain Jones make haste for Washington, New Hampshire?

EAGLE POND CEMETERY

Best-Maintained Cemetery in the State?

WILMOT

Public cemetery

On Route 4 heading west, 0.2 mile after New Canada Road. Grounds open dawn to dusk.

This is one of my favorite cemeteries, but then again I'm biased since I drive by it at least once a week. It's one of the best-maintained small cemeteries that I've seen. It has a prime location, on a little knoll on the east side of Route 4. This cemetery had better views than most houses built at the time it was established: the mid-nineteenth century. In those pre-snowplow days, most homes were built close to the road to provide easy access when the drifts grew higher than the house, which happened pretty often.

The stones are straight, bleached white as teeth, well taken care of, and they all face due west, just overlooking the railroad bed across the road where the Boston & Maine used to roar by.

You may first mistake the graveyard for a military cemetery. Each stone stands perfectly upright, and each row is in a straight line. Stand to the side and look up; you won't see a single degree of deviation.

Most of the graves in the first few rows closest to the road have footstones with the initials of the deceased carved into them. The only odd thing about the cemetery is that the inscriptions on the tombstones face to the west while the footstones are situated to the east. This marks out the approximate boundary of the casket that lies beneath the ground, but in order to read the inscriptions, you have to walk around to the other side of the stone. It was an unusual placement for the time.

The stones in Eagle Pond Cemetery stand with military precision.

A white picket fence gate serves as the entrance to the cemetery, and several of the graves hold markers for Civil War veterans.

From Head to Toe

TYPICALLY, GRAVE MARKERS INCLUDE A HEADSTONE AND A FOOTSTONE. IN ADDITION TO THE IDENTIFYING INFORMATION—NAME, AGE, AND DATE OF DEATH—THE HEADSTONE MAY INCLUDE AN EPITAPH AND VARIOUS DESIGNS AND ICONS. THE FOOTSTONE IS SIMPLER AND SMALLER. ALTHOUGH IT MAY HAVE THE NAME PLUS A SMALL DESIGN, OFTEN IT CONTAINS ONLY THE NAME, OR EVEN SIMPLY THE INITIALS.

LAUREL HILL CEMETERY

Site of the Meetinghouse Tragedy

WILTON

Public cemetery

*From Routes 101/31, head south on Abbott Hill
Road; the cemetery is 0.2 mile down the road.
Grounds open dawn to dusk.*

Wilton is yet another New Hampshire town that locals contend has more than its fair share of ghosts, especially in its cemeteries. While nearby Vale End Cemetery can boast of a particular ghost known as the Blue Lady—she shows up as a blue column of light hovering above the gravestone for Mary Ritter Spaulding in the northwest corner of the graveyard—the ghost who is purported to haunt Laurel Hill has no name and appears as a purple streak of light. Less often, a man dressed in nineteenth-century clothing shows up.

The reason for Wilton's prodigious numbers of ghost sightings, even today, could be the Meetinghouse Tragedy, which occurred near the town center in 1773. As was the custom back then, when colonists needed help raising a barn or building a home, their fellow townspeople would help out for a day or, more often, for a week or longer.

When the town needed a new meetinghouse to conduct town meetings in, the same rule applied, but this time there was a monetary reward tied in: Everyone who pitched in with the work received a reduction in the amount of property tax they had to pay to the town that year.

On a warm September morning, 120 men from the town signed on for the task. They worked for a good part of the day, but suddenly something went very wrong. One of the main support beams collapsed beneath the weight of both the construction materials and the men. Fifty-three men fell 27 feet to the floor joists below, with most injured severely; five did not survive. The town mourned their loss, and the meetinghouse eventually got built, but the grief that hung over the town for years may explain the numerous reported ghost sightings and hauntings around a number of the town's cemeteries dating back to that era.

RHODE ISLAND

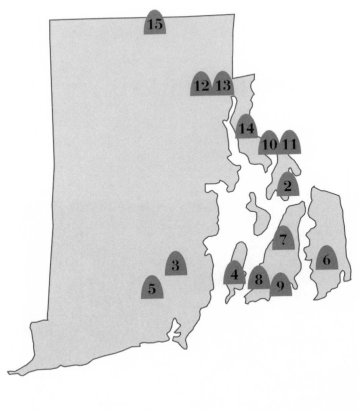

1 Block Island: Palatine Cemetery

2 Bristol: DeWolf Cemetery

3 Exeter: Chestnut Hill Baptist
Church Cemetery

4 Jamestown: Old Friends' Burial Ground

5 Kingstown: Platform Cemetery

6 Little Compton: Old Burying Ground

7 Middletown: Newport Memorial Park Cemetery

8 Newport: Common Burying Ground

9 Newport: Island Cemetery

10 Portsmouth: Bow-Wow Villa Cemetery

11 Portsmouth: St. Mary's Churchyard

12 Providence: North Burial Ground

13 Providence: Swan Point Cemetery

14 Tiverton: Pocasset Hill Cemetery

15 Woonsocket: Precious Blood Cemetery

PALATINE CEMETERY
Site of a Tragic Shipwreck

BLOCK ISLAND

Public cemetery

The corner of Cooneymus and Dickens Roads.
Grounds open dawn to dusk.

At Block Island's Palatine Cemetery, only one monument stands in the entire site. It's a memorial to the victims of the shipwreck of a vessel—and one on which the vast majority of the crew and passengers were near death even before the wreck; the crash was merely the tragic ending to a sad story.

What has come to be known as the *Palatine* was actually a ship with the name of *Herbert*. It was one of twelve Dutch ships filled with 3,200 passengers from the Rhineland section of Germany, who were eager to make new homes in the New World when it set sail from Rotterdam in December 1709. It didn't take long after launch for trouble to arise, however, first through a series of winter storms that delayed the voyage and altered the course of the trip, and second by a crew leaning toward mutiny and who had an iron grip on a hull full of food and supplies.

Prices for bread and water skyrocketed when the crew offered them to the wealthy passengers. Though accounts differ, historians do concur that the captain was murdered, the crew abandoned ship in the midst of violent storms, and the passengers could do little until the ship eventually ran aground. It landed just off Block Island, and though people on the island did attempt to save some of the passengers, the rough conditions prevented all of them from escaping to dry land. The islanders set fire to the vessel, a common way to warn approaching ships of its presence.

As the men headed back to the island, they heard a bloodcurdling scream come from the direction of the ship. The scream came from a wealthy woman who, driven mad by the voyage, had stayed on the ship when everyone else fled. It was said that she refused to leave her belongings behind. Local legend has it that every year on July 7, the anniversary of the shipwreck, the ghost of the *Palatine* appears just off the coast of Block Island. If you listen carefully, you'll hear a woman screaming.

A Fish Story

HE'S DONE A'CATCHING COD
AND GONE TO MEET HIS GOD.
—Fisherman's epitaph on
Block Island, Rhode Island

DEWOLF CEMETERY

A Colorful Past

BRISTOL

Public cemetery

*Woodlawn Avenue, 0.3 mile in from Metacom
Avenue. Grounds open dawn to dusk.*

The DeWolf Cemetery is an unusual example of an old New England family cemetery that it is still relatively intact and cared for; most family cemeteries are found in remote locations and are poorly maintained or often abandoned.

Captain James DeWolf, who was born in 1764 and died in 1837, lived among the wealthy barons of Bristol in a huge mansion on—what else?—DeWolf Avenue. One day he decided to build a deer park in a quiet corner of Bristol, on the southern end of town. He was so pleased with it that he decided he wanted to spend eternity there, and so instead of attracting deer to the site, he opted to turn it into a cemetery for the members of his family. He instructed his workers to construct a mound of dirt 20 feet high that would serve as his eventual tomb, with the mandate that an iron door serve as the entrance. According to local historians, the captain offered as his rationale: "As long as any of [my children] are around, you'll see my gold teeth, even when the rest of us is dust."

Today, sadly, the door is gone, and a tree is growing up through the middle of the "mound" of dirt that was designed to be as magnificent a structure as DeWolf's mansion. In 1842 a grave robber named John Dickinson broke into the tomb and stole the captain's gold teeth, along with a few other items, including a casket plate. It seemed that

Dickinson made casket snatching his livelihood around Bristol, though he tended to leave the bodies behind for medical schools . . . but that's another story.

The intrepid Dickinson was caught and executed in 1855 for the litany of grave robbing he had conducted over the years, which meant that there was a very good chance that his corpse ended up lying on a cold slab in a nearby medical school, eager students standing by with scalpels in their hands. Indeed, this was the common fate of executed prisoners back in the day.

The DeWolf Cemetery grew from its first interment of the captain. Today almost three dozen other DeWolfs lie beside their forebear for eternity.

CHESTNUT HILL BAPTIST CHURCH CEMETERY

Vampires in New England

EXETER

Public cemetery

*On the north side of Route 102 between
Sunderland Road and Locust Valley Road.
Grounds open dawn to dusk.*

Vampirism has long played a part in New England history, but perhaps one of the most notorious cases concerns Mercy Brown, a nineteen-year-old girl who died in Exeter, Rhode Island, in 1892. Whether she was actually a vampire or the family just had a particularly long run of bad luck is not clear. Here's the story so you can decide for yourself.

When Mercy Brown died in January of that year, she was the third family member to die within a matter of months. The surviving family members started to suspect that something was not quite right, and one suggested that the quick and frequent deaths were the signs of a vampire, dead or alive, in their ranks.

They decided that unless they took action, another death would befall the family before long. They opted to start their investigation with the dead members of the Brown family. The first two deceased family members were exhumed, and they were discovered to be skeletons, decomposing properly as real humans should. When they dug up Mercy, however, they found that she had not decomposed at all; in fact, she still had fresh blood in her veins.

The verdict was unanimous: Mercy was the suspected vampire, and she had to be completely vanquished so that no more family members would die. They removed her heart and burned it. The vampire exorcism ritual back then demanded, in part, that the surviving family members consume the ash, and so they did, at graveside. The Browns subsequently re-interred Mercy's body.

It's believed that the exorcism worked, because no more members of the Brown family died unexpectedly. However, ghost chasers report that strange lights are sometimes seen wandering in the vicinity of Mercy's tombstone.

Mercy Brown was exhumed for a vampire exorcism, then reburied.

OLD FRIENDS' BURIAL GROUND

Final Resting Place of Captain
"One-Gun" Eldred

JAMESTOWN

Public cemetery

On the south side of Route 138 near Helm Street.
Grounds open dawn to dusk.

Jamestown, Rhode Island, which takes up all of Conanicut Island, sits in Narragansett Bay about 17 miles south of Providence. It's famous for two things: First, that it was settled by Quakers, aka the Society of Friends, a religious group that preaches nonviolence; and second, that it was home to John Eldred, a Revolutionary War patriot who gained a certain notoriety whenever he saw a British warship approaching his stakeout point on the island. Operating with just one cannon, Captain Eldred nonetheless was able to take aim at the British vessels with such frequency and ferocity that the redcoat navy believed they were facing a veritable army of colonists.

Word obviously spread among the British like wildfire that they were to use extreme caution when making the passage in the vicinity of Jamestown. After a while the Brits decided to take action, and on December 10, 1775, they landed in Jamestown intending to destroy the artillery company they thought was firing upon their ships. They were quite surprised to discover not only that the barrage of fire was coming from just one cannon, but also that the man who was unleashing ammunition upon their ships with such fury was actually sixty-three years old! Captain Eldred's post was known as the One-Gun Battery.

Tilted gravestones are a common sight in New England, given the havoc winter plays upon the land.

In retaliation, the British went on a rampage of destruction on the island, which caused many of the townspeople to flee to the mainland, specifically Newport, until the war was over.

In the cemetery, Captain "One-Gun" Eldred's grave is surrounded by those of Revolutionary War soldiers and early settlers of Jamestown and contained by a stone wall.

PLATFORM CEMETERY
Left Behind in the Name of Progress

KINGSTOWN

Public cemetery

Shermantown Road, 1 mile west of Routes 1/138.
Grounds open dawn to dusk.

People are often amazed to compare photographs or paintings of certain regions of New England that are a hundred or so years apart. For instance, in 1850, New England was not as heavily forested as it is today; in New Hampshire, where logging was a primary industry, the land was 85 percent cleared. Today it is 85 percent forested.

Similarly, people are often surprised to discover that just because a church or town building is 300 years old, it doesn't mean the structure spent every one of those 300 years in the same place. Buildings and even entire neighborhoods were frequently moved to take advantage of a location that didn't flood or a village that would be closer to a new railroad line that was coming through. Oxen were the preferred mode of transportation for these buildings.

The same went for cemeteries, including the Platform Cemetery in the town of North Kingstown. Before it was a cemetery, it was the site of St. Paul's Church, built in 1707. Almost a full century later, the church building, steeple and all, was moved 5.5 miles to the town of Wickford; incredibly, the trip took only one week.

After the church left, the churchyard cemetery was still used for new burials, though admittedly, they didn't occur with the frequency they had when the church was adjacent to the graveyard.

OLD BURYING GROUND

Final Resting Place for
First White Female Born in New England

LITTLE COMPTON

Public cemetery

At the center of Little Compton, on the commons.
Grounds open dawn to dusk.

Little Compton's Old Burying Ground contains a few stones that intrigue and raise a few questions of passersby—but really, isn't that the attraction of every older graveyard?

One gravestone marks the final resting place of Benjamin Church, a prominent leader in the battle against the Native Americans during King Philip's War. Later on, Church switched sides and was one of the earliest colonists to lead a fight against the British Crown during the battle named the Great Swamp Fight in 1675. The next year he was the force behind the death of King Philip, sparking a century-long conflict between the colonists and British royalty that wouldn't end until after the Revolution.

One of the more prominent monuments at the burial ground is the site for Elisabeth Pabodie, the daughter of John and Priscilla Alden; she was the first white female born in New England. Her tombstone was erected after her death in 1717, of course, but later on it was encompassed by a large granite obelisk that lists her distinction, something the gravestone didn't point out.

Not far from Elisabeth's grave site is the plot for the Palmer family, specifically the stones for Simeon and his wives. On one side of Simeon the stone reads:

LIDIA THE WIFE OF MR. SIMEON PALMER, D. 1754 AE. 35

On the other side you'll find another stone with the inscription:

ELIZABETH WHO SHOULD HAVE BEEN THE WIFE OF MR. SIMEON PALMER, D. 1776 AE 64.

However, the import of the story is somewhat altered when historians of the town point out that Elizabeth did end up marrying Simeon after Lidia's death. What do you think the mystery of the stone is?

NEWPORT MEMORIAL PARK CEMETERY

Garden of Angels

MIDDLETOWN

Public cemetery

123 Howland Avenue.
Grounds open dawn to dusk.

If you've been a taphophile for years, then you know that some people understand what you're about in a second, while others will look at you strangely and imagine that if you had your way, you'd dress all in black and have numerous body piercings.

Even people who love cemeteries, whether for their historical value or because it's the one quiet place they know they can go for peace and reflection, sometimes have different experiences at the same cemetery, even on the same day. Most would attribute the variances to ghosts, or lack thereof. At the Newport Memorial Cemetery in Middletown, if you've spent any amount of time in town at all, you've probably heard about the crying babies in the part of the graveyard known as the Garden of Angels. More than twenty infants have been buried in this section in the last half century alone, and some say that if you happen to be walking through the section either at midnight, or on a night with a full moon, you'll hear the crying as plain as day.

This cemetery is also distinctive because it embodies a trend that is fairly common: It was built near or adjacent to a small family burial yard. The Taggart Burial Ground is accessed via a private road approximately 130 feet east of the entrance to the park. Continue on this road until you reach a stone wall on your left, and follow along the wall until you come to a gate. Enter the gate and cross over to the southwest corner of the field to find the Taggart cemetery, which contains ten gravestones that date from 1818.

Little Lambs: Children's Memorials

THIS EPITAPH, FROM OLD BURIAL GROUND IN MARBLEHEAD, MASSACHUSETTS, IS TYPICAL OF THOSE THAT WERE INSCRIBED ON CHILDREN'S TOMBSTONES:

IN MEMORY OF
RUTHY FREEMAN INGALLS
DAUGR. OF MR. WILLIAM
& MRS. MARGARET INGALLS
WHO DIED JULY 26. 1797,
AGED 3 WEEKS & 1 DAY.

GOD GIVES US COMFORTS &
RETURNS THE SAND
HIS WILL BE DONE & BLESSED BE
HIS NAME.

COMMON BURYING GROUND

Final Resting Place of
African-American Colonists

NEWPORT

Public cemetery

At the corner of Farewell and Warner Streets.
From Broadway, head north on Farewell Street
for blocks until you reach Warner Street. Grounds
open dawn to dusk.

Newport has a wealth of burial grounds with rich histories scattered throughout the city. The ten-acre Common Burying Ground, founded in 1640 initially as a final resting place for strangers, is particularly distinctive due to the large section that was set aside for Newport's black population, both free and slave.

Newport had a large population of African Americans in the 1700s, an indication of the amount of trade that was conducted in the wealthy port town in those days. In fact, Newport was the sole stop in North America for many ships that traveled a triangular trade route from Africa's west coast to the Caribbean islands and on to the New World. Of course, the cargo included both foodstuffs such as rum and molasses and human cargo in the form of slaves. In colonial days slavery was as prevalent in New England as in the South, and Newport masters ran plantations much as their counterparts in Georgia did.

The black section of the graveyard is north of Dyre Avenue, and though the carved angel faces that appear on the stones of eighteenth-century vintage are identical to those in the "white" sections, the primary difference is that in most cases, no firm date of birth is given; most

Flowers symbolize the fragility of life.

Africans born into slavery did not know their birthdays, nor did their owners. This is reflected on stones that list the date of death, typically followed by "aged about 64 years." Another sign is that the term *beloved servant* often appears in inscriptions. The word *Negro* is also common. Perhaps one of the most heartbreaking stones reads:

> ANN A NEGRO CHILD BELONGING TO MR. ROBERT OLIVER &
> DAUGHTER TO HIS NEGRO MIMBO AGED 2 Y DIED JUNE 1743.

As was often the case, the last name was not listed on the stone.

ISLAND CEMETERY

Burial Spot of Heroes & Millionaires

NEWPORT

Public cemetery

*Warner Street, next to the Common Burying
Ground. Grounds open dusk to dawn.*

While the focus of its neighbor the Common Burying Ground is the eighteenth century, take one step into the Island Cemetery and you fast-forward one hundred years. In fact, Island Cemetery is said to be representative of the two most common residents of Newport: millionaires and naval heroes.

First, the millionaires. August Belmont has what is possibly the largest and most elaborate grave site at the cemetery, which is nothing to shake a stick at. Belmont became the head of the family banking establishment upon his father's death, and at the age of thirty-seven, August proceeded to spin the family fortune of $25 million into gold by investing in the New York subway, among other accomplishments. On the side he ran the America's Cup, bred racehorses—yes, New York's Belmont Park is named after him—and just happened to marry the daughter of Commander Matthew C. Perry, one of the aforementioned naval heroes. Look for the Roman arch guarded by two toga-clad women.

Matthew Perry and his equally illustrious brother Commodore Oliver Perry are also buried here, in the vicinity of August's monument. Both brothers fought in the War of 1812, but Oliver died of yellow fever on a diplomatic trip to Trinidad seven years later. Matthew went on to preside over the 1853 naval standoff with Japan that resulted in the opening of trade between the United States and that country, but like Oliver, he died away from home in New York at the age of sixty-four. After initial burial in other cemeteries, the bodies of both brothers were ultimately returned to the family plot at Island Cemetery.

Other millionaires buried at Island Cemetery include the Auchincloss family, an institution in Newport society. The patriarch of the family, Hugh, had a stepdaughter named Jacqueline Bouvier, who later added the name Kennedy. Another family member was the architect Richard Morris Hunt, who designed a number of Newport's more illustrious mansions, including the Breakers. The Auchincloss plot is located near the chapel on the eastern side of the cemetery.

BOW-WOW VILLA CEMETERY

Gone to the Dogs

PORTSMOUTH

Public cemetery

837 Wapping Road. From Route 138, head east on Sandy Point Avenue for 0.25 mile, then go south on Wapping Road for about 1 mile. Grounds open dawn to dusk. (401) 847–1655.

Here's a bit of useless trivia for you: Where did the Duke and Duchess of Windsor bury their late, much-lamented pug dog? None other than Portsmouth, Rhode Island, in the Bow-Wow Villa Cemetery.

Though pet cemeteries have become more common through the years as many people have come to regard cats, dogs, and other critters as bona fide members of the family, back in the days of the Great Depression, it was highly unusual to hold a funeral and burial service for an animal. The year 1938, however, marked the founding of the Bow-Wow Villa, which also serves as a kennel and grooming facility for animals while they're still walking around.

In any case, this is a graveyard that is better cared for than many cemeteries for people. Many of the "residents" of the cemetery lived their former life in the palatial mansions of Newport and Block Island, and it shows: Just take a look at the attention to detail on the elaborately carved headstones, the engraved likenesses of beloved pets, and even the types of pets that are buried here—from ferrets to parrots and everything in between.

The Duke and Duchess of Windsor are probably a good model of the bereaved owners who have laid their furry friends to rest here, though they may have taken the passion for their pets a bit to extremes: They took their dogs everywhere with them and also employed a personal chef and a human pooper scooper to take care of the more unsavory side of loving such a royal dog.

At Death's Door

TAKING A DEAD PERSON OUT OF A HOUSE, TENT OR HUT THROUGH THE USUAL EXIT WAS THOUGHT TO BE DANGEROUS. PEOPLE BELIEVED THE DEAD MUST NOT USE THE SAME DOOR AS THE LIVING, OR THE SICKNESS MIGHT RUB OFF ON THE DOORWAY. SOME PEOPLE EVEN BUILT SPECIAL DOORS IN THEIR HOUSES FOR THE DEAD. SUCH DOORS, IN OLD ITALY AND DENMARK, KEPT THE REGULAR DOORWAY FREE FROM THE INFECTION OF THE DEAD.

—Ann Warren Turner, *Houses for the Dead*

ST. MARY'S CHURCHYARD

Grave Site of a Dedicated Yachtsman

PORTSMOUTH

Public cemetery

324 East Main Road (Route 138).
Grounds open dawn to dusk.

The name *Vanderbilt* has been paired with Newport, Rhode Island, for more decades than anyone would care to count.

However, since Newport was officially the family's second-home address, most of the Vanderbilts preferred to spend their eternal rest in their plot in Moravian Cemetery in Staten Island, New York. Except for Harold Stirling Vanderbilt, who was born on July 6, 1884, and died on July 4, 1970. Harold served as a director of the New York Central Railroad from 1913 through 1954; one of his idle-hour pastimes was to invent the game of contract bridge.

But instead of preferring to be known as a considerable force at the railroad or the inventor of a new kind of card game, Harold wanted to be known as a yachtsman first and foremost, undoubtedly the primary reason behind his choice of burial place. Harold won the America's Cup international yachting competition in 1930 and again in 1934 and 1937. In fact, a copy of a yachtsman's wheel, which Harold called, simply, "the Wheel," is carved on his tombstone, in the southwest section of the cemetery near the driveway.

Harold died hours before the 1970 America's Cup race was to begin. To honor his passing, most of the boats and ships in Newport Harbor lowered their flags to half-mast that day.

NORTH BURIAL GROUND

Oldest Cemetery in Providence

PROVIDENCE

Public cemetery

Take Exit 23 off I-95. Follow Industrial Drive west to Route 122 north. The cemetery is a few blocks ahead. Grounds open dawn to dusk.

When residents were first settling a town in colonial times, they sometimes looked upon public acreage with an eye toward establishing it as what we would think of as multipurpose land today. For example, not only did town commons serve as places for townspeople to gather, but many commons also had small burial yards in one corner while an animal pound sat in the opposite corner.

Not only was the North Burial Ground the first public cemetery established in Providence, but it was also designated to serve as a "training field and for other public uses" in its first year of use, 1700. Some of those "other uses" include serving as the second resting place for those who were buried in other Rhode Island cemeteries, since many stones were moved here from graveyards in surrounding towns throughout the 1800s.

Since the North Burial Ground is Providence's oldest, a number of prominent Rhode Islanders are buried here, including Stephen Hopkins, who died in 1785. Hopkins served as governor of the Rhode Island colony for ten terms, and he was also one of the original signers of the Declaration of Independence.

The founder of Brown University—which was first named Rhode Island College—was one Nicholas Brown, and he was buried here in

1841. Horace Mann, often called the Father of American Public Education since he established the first public school system in Boston, was laid to rest here as well. Though they were not his official last words, the month before he died, Mann gave a commencement speech at Antioch College, which he founded, and in his address he told his students to "Be ashamed to die until you have won some victory for humanity."

Finally, a simple stone in a quiet corner of the cemetery marks the grave of Charles Henry Dow, the founder of the *Wall Street Journal.*

SWAN POINT CEMETERY

Providence's Garden Cemetery

PROVIDENCE

Public cemetery

*585 Blackstone Boulevard. Grounds open
8:00 A.M.–5:00 P.M. during Standard Time, and
8:00 A.M.–7:00 P.M. during Daylight Saving.
(401) 272–1314; www.swanpointcemetery.com.
A map is available at the Web site.*

Swan Point is generally regarded as the premier cemetery in Rhode Island. The cemetery was founded as a forty-acre tract in 1846, and like Mount Auburn in Cambridge, Massachusetts, and Green-Wood in Brooklyn, New York, Swan Point was initially designed to capture the Victorian vogue of treating cemeteries as public parks, enabling Sunday picnics and strolls with the entire family in tow. Many of the older grave markers reflect this sensibility, with marble benches and miniature bronze temples scattered throughout the grounds.

Time hasn't changed much here, except that visitors who are not attending a funeral are more likely to be walking or jogging than sitting beneath a parasol.

Some famous permanent residents of Swan Point include erotica writer Anaïs Nin, along with H. P. Lovecraft, the horror writer. Lovecraft fans gather at his grave each year on or around the anniversary of his death—March 15—to commemorate his work. Attendees say that Lovecraft himself often appears in the form of "something strange" at these gatherings. One year it was a cackle of crows loudly

Fans of horror writer H. P. Lovecraft meet at his grave on the
anniversary of his death.

accompanying the spoken tributes, while another year it was an unex-
pected snow squall.

Although Swan Point was not his first resting place, one other
famous resident at the cemetery is Major Sullivan Ballou, the Civil War
soldier who was killed in the first Battle of Bull Run but forever memorialized by his "My Dear Sarah" letter featured in Ken Burns's PBS doc-
umentary *The Civil War*. Ballou was initially buried in Sudley Church,
Virginia, near the scene of the carnage. His Union comrades later dug
up his body and transported it to Swan Point. His beloved Sarah, who
never remarried, died in 1917 at the age of eighty-one and was buried
beside her husband.

POCASSET HILL CEMETERY

Buried with a Favorite Car

TIVERTON

Public cemetery

Follow Routes 138/28 to Exit 5. Head north on Route 138 for about 1 mile; the cemetery is on your right. Grounds open dawn to dusk.

Do you harbor a secret desire to disprove the old adage "You can't take it with you"? If so, then Rose Martin's story will intrigue you.

Rose Martin was eighty-four years old when she died in 1998. She had spent many of her years in the small Rhode Island town of Tiverton, near the Massachusetts border. Though Rose had been a police matron in the town, and she loved her neighbors and her husband, her first love was her 1962 Corvair. The people of the town had grown accustomed to seeing Rose cruise around the streets of Tiverton, and despite Ralph Nader's criticism of the model back in the 1960s, Mrs. Martin actually used the Corvair as her daily vehicle for an astounding thirty-six years.

It was her wish to be buried in the Corvair when her time came. Perhaps her fellow Tivertonians knew Rose too well, for they honored her request.

A few interesting asides: The car, though it was far from being one of the land yachts that were common in that era, required four burial plots to fit into the ground. At the burial, Rose's casket was accompanied by six uniformed officers acting as pallbearers. The engine—which was in the rear compartment of the car—was removed for environmental reasons and also because it was the only way to move a casket into the interior without having to remove the window pillar. And so, just before burial, the six policemen slid the casket into the car, and the entire package was slowly lowered into the ground.

Today, to look at the plot—look for a tombstone that looks like an oversized Bible with MARTIN written on it—you'd never know that a car lies beneath your feet. But you'll sure know where Rose's priorities were: While the stone displays a photo of Rose and her Corvair, a picture of her husband, who is buried beside her, is nowhere to be found.

PRECIOUS BLOOD CEMETERY

Burial Site of a Would-Be Saint

WOONSOCKET

Public cemetery

Take Route 114 west from Mendon Road. Cross over Route 126; the cemetery is 1 block ahead. Grounds open dawn to dusk.

Judging from the tour buses and crowds that still throng a particular grave site at Woonsocket's Precious Blood Cemetery, you wouldn't be far off the mark to wonder which rock star was buried here.

Marie Rose Ferron, who was born in 1902 and died in 1936, was a veritable celebrity in the strictly religious sense: She is reputed to be the only person ever born in New England who exhibited stigmata marks—that is, lesions approximating the crucifixion wounds of Jesus—on her forehead, hands, and feet. Marie Rose was extremely religious, and she suffered from a particularly debilitating form of arthritis from birth. When she was a child, she visited a Canadian monk who administered hands-on healing to her limbs. From that point on, stigmata marks began to spontaneously appear on her body, and once word got out, the crowds of religious faithful couldn't stay away.

Pilgrims came from all over the world in the hope that Marie Rose, in turn, would heal their physical wounds and foretell the second coming of Jesus. They hailed her as a mystic and a religious visionary, capable of bringing about miracles. Her followers even appealed to the Vatican to consider her for sainthood. Even though a bishop conducted several inquiries into Marie Rose's gifts, he declined conferring sainthood on her, though a throng of faithful are still campaigning for it.

Today her followers visit her grave to pray and to take away a little bit of the earth that covers the site, which they view as still holding the power to perform miracles. They also pay a visit to the Little Rose Family Chapel at 302 Providence Street in Woonsocket, where her family lived after Marie Rose's death; at the time of her passing, the family lived at 271 Providence Street, where people hoping for a miracle stand on the sidewalk in front of the house to say a prayer.

Vermont

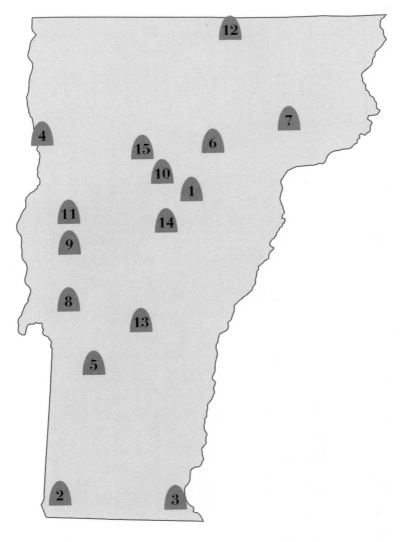

1 Barre: Hope Cemetery

2 Bennington: Old Bennington Cemetery

3 Brattleboro: Prospect Hill Cemetery

4 Burlington: Greenmount Cemetery

5 Cuttingsville: Laurel Glen Cemetery

6 East Calais: Fairview Cemetery

7 Lyndon Center: Lyndon Center Cemetery

8 Mendon: Civil War Horse Grave

9 Middlebury: West Cemetery

10 Montpelier: Green Mount Cemetery

11 New Haven: Evergreen Cemetery

12 Newport: St. Mary's Cemetery

13 Plymouth: Notch Cemetery

14 Randolph: Randolph Center Cemetery

15 Waterbury: Ben & Jerry's Flavor Graveyard

HOPE CEMETERY

A Stonecutters' Gallery

BARRE

Public cemetery

*Route 14, north of Route 302. From downtown
Barre, take Route 14 north for 1 mile; the cemetery
is on your left. Grounds open dawn to dusk.*
(802) 476–6245

Barre has been home to thousands of immigrants over the years, from the Italian stonecutters who came to Vermont via Ellis Island to work in the granite quarries, to the Irishmen who were recruited in droves to work on the railroad, first to lay track and then to operate the trains.

The granite quarries were founded shortly after the end of the War of 1812. Three grades of granite are still mined from the mountains: a coarse stone ideal for millstones and doorsteps; a less sandy stone for house foundations, much like the stone used to build the state capitol in Montpelier; and the beautiful, almost flawless stone that is used for gravestones and monuments all over the world, including right here in Hope Cemetery in Barre, Vermont.

Hope Cemetery is a seventy-five-acre burial ground that dates back to 1895 and is known for its elaborate carvings by Vermont's turn-of-the-twentieth-century stonecutters. New stones are interspersed with old ones, and Italian names are plentiful.

The lifelike sculptures of some of the grave markers are the main attraction at Hope Cemetery. Far left and at the back of the cemetery, look for the Brusa stone: A brooding angel, hand on chin, legs crossed, trumpet on lap, sits beneath a Greek pillar and balustrade sculpture.

Till death do us part: Gwendolyn and William Halvosa

Also look for Elia Corti's stone, a life-sized monument at the crossroads near the back of the cemetery. Corti was a stonecutter who died in 1903. His stone shows his full-sized likeness sitting and gazing at the mountains.

Another monument—located in another patch of stories downhill and secluded from the main yard—depicts a wife comforting her dying husband, who succumbed to silicosis, a lung disease many stonecutters contracted from breathing in the stone dust. And directly in front is a sculpture of Gwendolyn and William Halvosa, a husband and wife holding hands, sitting up in bed, with the inscription:

SET ME AS A SEAL UPON THINE HEART
FOR LOVE IS STRONG AS DEATH.

Heading back out of the cemetery, pull over and check out the stones where you see the soccer ball stone. Look for a chair that serves as a grave marker, another with a classic Green Mountain view—

complete with fence posts, rifle, fishing rod, dune buggy, and lots of trucks. One shows a Shell Oil truck driving through the mountains; another serves as a belated advertisement for the Benedini Well Company, depicting a truck in the process of digging an artesian well.

OLD BENNINGTON CEMETERY
Robert Frost's Grave Site

BENNINGTON

Public cemetery

*On Route 9, 1 mile west of the town center, behind
the First Congregational Church. Grounds open
dawn to dusk.*

Though just about every New England state has laid claim to the poet
Robert Frost at one time or another, the truth is that he chose Vermont
to be his final resting place—specifically Bennington, where his family
plot was located.

Frost died in Boston in 1963 and was cremated in Cambridge,
Massachusetts. After memorial services at both Harvard and Amherst
College, his ashes were transported back to Vermont for burial in the
historic Old Bennington Cemetery. Not only are numerous soldiers of
the Revolutionary War buried here but the cemetery lies in the shadow
of the Bennington Battle Monument, erected to honor the Battle of
Bennington, the decisive fight in which Ethan Allen's Green Mountain
Boys defeated the British in August 1777.

In addition, no less than five of Vermont's governors are buried in
the Old Bennington Cemetery. Most of these gravestones are utilitarian
in nature, reflecting the times and the inherent seriousness of military
leaders and soldiers, and it's fitting that Frost's stone follows in the
same vein. Besides his name and dates of birth and death, it features a
simple epitaph, which Frost wrote himself:

I HAD A LOVER'S QUARREL WITH THE WORLD.

Old Bennington Cemetery

In contrast, some of the stones that date from just after the Revolutionary War and the time when Vermont became the fourteenth state are unusually elaborate and decorative, given the no-nonsense nature of the times.

PROSPECT HILL CEMETERY
Final Resting Place of "Jubilee Jim" Fisk

BRATTLEBORO

Public cemetery

From Route 9, take Route 5 south. Head south on Elm Street, which turns into Prospect Street, then into South Main Street. The cemetery is 1 block down on the left. Grounds open dawn to dusk.

The otherwise peaceful and entirely run-of-the-mill Prospect Hill Cemetery in the southeastern corner of Vermont contains the grave of a notorious robber baron who riled Wall Street and amused fellow native Vermonters with his various exploits before, during, and after the Civil War.

Colonel James Fisk—nicknamed the "Improbable Rascal" in addition to "Jubilee Jim"—was born in nearby tiny North Pownal, but from an early age it was clear that he was destined for larger things, not all of them legal. Historians suppose this was not a surprise, given the fact that he was born on April Fool's Day in 1834 as well as his early dabblings in circus life as a bona fide ringmaster. Fisk got his start by illegally buying and selling cotton in the Confederate states for buyers in the North and by offering Confederate bonds to brokers in England. He then moved his talents to Wall Street where, with the help of fellow robber baron Jay Gould, he "stole" the Erie Railroad from the esteemed Cornelius Vanderbilt through sketchy economic maneuvers. For his next act he tried to take control of the gold market, resulting in the first Black Friday Wall Street had known.

But he is perhaps best known for the scandal that arose when he took up with actress Josie Mansfield. The ensuing, messy love triangle ended with his murder at the age of thirty-seven. His funeral was a colossal gathering, with tens of thousands of New Yorkers paying respect followed by a military procession to lead his casket to the railway car that would bring him home to Brattleboro.

His monument in the southern corner of the cemetery accurately captures the flamboyance and sheer gall of the man when alive: On each of the four corners of the tall monument perch four elaborately carved women, naked from the waist up and holding a portion of Fisk's lost empire. Two hold large books titled *Railroads* and *Steamboats*, while a third holds a large sack of coins, representing Commerce. The last exemplifies the Stage, which was, of course, what eventually did Fisk in.

Showing Off

THEY SEEMED TO RESERVE FOR THESE GLOOMY
TRIBUTES THEIR SOLE ATTEMPT AT FACETIOUSNESS.
—Alice Morse Earle, nineteenth-century historian,
on those who wrote inscriptions for tombstones

GREENMOUNT CEMETERY

Ethan Allen's Grave Site

BURLINGTON

Public cemetery

*From Exit 14 west off I–89, head onto Route 2 west.
Turn right onto East Avenue, then make another
right turn onto Colchester Avenue. The cemetery is a
few blocks ahead on the right. Grounds open dawn
to dusk.*

Undoubtedly the most famous resident of Burlington's largest cemetery is Ethan Allen, one of the original Green Mountain Boys, along with his brother Ira and other patriots of the day. Ethan made his mark in Vermont in the late 1700s, when both New York and New Hampshire were fighting over the territory that the Allen brothers had christened Vermont, which they claimed was a state independent of any other—and of any other country, for that matter.

Though Ira went on to found the University of Vermont, his brother was the more famous of the siblings; besides, Ira is buried in an unmarked grave in a Quaker cemetery in Philadelphia, after enduring capture by the British, imprisonment in Vermont for debt, and spending his remaining years living in poverty in Philadelphia. A small obelisk does mark his memory in Greenmount Cemetery and stands next to his brother's. At 42 feet high, Ethan's monument towers over Ira's modest marker, an embodiment of the same overshadowing that occurred in the brothers' lives.

Ethan Allen's accomplishments are listed
on his obelisk.

Beside Ethan's towering grave marker, in the middle of the cemetery, stands an 8-foot-high statue of his likeness with arms raised—
doubtless what the stonecarver thought he looked like at the moment
of his greatest achievement, when Ethan demanded the surrender of
Fort Ticonderoga "in the name of the Great Jehovah and the
Continental Congress." On Ethan's mammoth obelisk, a list of his various feats is inscribed on all four sides of the shaft.

Today everything from companies to parks is named after Ethan
Allen. Schoolchildren and visitors alike know his name as part of the
heritage and history of Vermont. The monuments to his memory—and
to his brother—are fitting memorials.

LAUREL GLEN CEMETERY

Monument from a Grief-Stricken Man

CUTTINGSVILLE

Public cemetery

*From the intersection of Routes 140 and 155 in
East Wallingford, head north on Route 103 for 3
miles. The cemetery is on the left.
Grounds open dawn to dusk.*

If you've already visited Hope Cemetery in Barre, you may think that it's the only place in Vermont to find such poignant expressions on the faces of the mourning statues. While Hope Cemetery does showcase the largest collection of a variety of stonecutters' work in one place, a statue in the little village of Cuttingsville, in the south-central part of the state, can compete with the best that the craftsmen farther north had to offer.

It is the Bowman mausoleum, a mammoth granite and marble tomb that closely resembles a Grecian temple. It towers over the road and dwarfs all else in the Laurel Glen Cemetery where it rests. But that's not the main attraction; the statue of John P. Bowman himself is.

Bowman was a wealthy man who lived across the street with his wife and young daughter in a luxurious—for the time, at least—mansion. Tragedy hit in the winter of 1879, when his wife and daughter both died within a short time. Bowman was grief-stricken. The only way he could work out his sorrow was to commission a fitting memorial to his lost family that would also project his great loss.

Bowman hired a top New York designer to craft the mausoleum so he could show the world how he felt. A total of 125 workers toiled

The completed Bowman mausoleum

John Bowman, grief-stricken over the loss of his wife and daughter, both depicted inside the tomb

away on the mausoleum and sculpture during 1881; $75,000 and one full year later, the job was done. The statue of Bowman so perfectly conveys the feeling of loss that it's hard to tear your eyes away from it. Bowman is portrayed leaning up against the entrance to the tomb, hat resting below one hand while he holds a memorial wreath in the other. He is shown gazing into the open door of the tomb with a look on his face that makes it clear he wants to join the others but knows that at least for now, he can't. This is particularly communicated by his free hand, which holds a key aimed toward the door.

The interior of the tomb shows marble busts of Bowman and his wife along with marble floors and walls, even chairs. The interior is well kept since it is closed each winter, and Bowman left a trust fund to pay for perpetual care. The fourth casket inside the tomb is that of an infant daughter, whom Bowman lost years before the loss of his wife and second daughter.

Reincarnation Tips

PEOPLE BUILT TOMBS OR GRAVES EITHER TO TRAP THE SPIRIT OR TO RELEASE IT QUICKLY AND SAFELY INTO THE NEXT WORLD. SOME CULTURES BELIEVED THESE SOULS WOULD BE REBORN IN THE NEXT BABY OF THE FAMILY. PEOPLE OF THE NEAR EAST SOMETIMES BURIED THEIR DEAD CHILDREN UNDER THE HOUSE FLOOR; THEN THEY WOULD BE NEAR FOR THEIR REBIRTH. ALGONQUIN INDIANS PUT THEIR DEAD YOUNG ONES BY THE ROADSIDE. THEN THE SOULS MIGHT ENTER PASS-ING WOMEN AND BE REBORN AS THEIR BABIES.

—Ann Warren Turner, *Houses for the Dead*

FAIRVIEW CEMETERY

A Confederate Yankee

EAST CALAIS

Public cemetery

From Route 2 in Plainfield, head north on Route 14 for about 8 miles. At East Calais, turn right onto Marshfield Road. Continue for 0.5 mile; the cemetery is at the intersection of Luce Road. Grounds open dawn to dusk.

You're taking a nice easy stroll through the Fairview Cemetery in peaceful East Calais, Vermont, when all of a sudden you think you must be seeing things. For what appears in front you but a handsome tombstone topped with—a Confederate flag? And not only a flag, but a Confederate marker to boot!

You can rub your eyes all you want, and you'll still see the distinctive red flag waved by the southern army during the Civil War. Most people don't realize that more than a handful of soldiers simply switched sides and fought for what should have been their enemy during the War Between the States. There were numerous reasons why this happened: Perhaps the Yankee had been living south of the Mason Dixon line for some time and began to identify more with southerners than his northern kin, or maybe he just empathized with the struggle of the South and joined the Confederate army to help out.

Whatever the reason, Melvin Dwinnell—whose tombstone is the one adorned with the Stars and Bars—was born in East Calais, Vermont, in 1825. After he graduated from the University of Vermont in 1849, he accepted a position as a teacher with the state of Georgia.

He also published a newspaper out of Rome, Georgia, and it's clear that after spending more than a decade living in the South, Dwinnell's sympathies lay more with people in his current life than with those in his northern birthplace. By the time the Civil War rolled around, he served with the Eighth Georgia Infantry Regiment before being injured at Gettysburg. After recovering from his injuries, he returned to the battlefield but cut his enlistment short in order to serve in the Georgia State Legislature.

He died in 1887 in Georgia, but his Vermont family obviously retained the last word by shipping his body back to his boyhood home for burial in Fairview Cemetery.

LYNDON CENTER CEMETERY

Last Word from an Atheist

LYNDON CENTER

Public cemetery

Route 122, across the street from the Lyndon Center Post Office. Grounds open dawn to dusk.

Like the Old Burying Ground in Milford, New Hampshire, and the Old German Cemetery in Waldoboro, Maine, the Lyndon Center Cemetery in Vermont's Northeast Kingdom includes a stone to mark the grave of a man who just had to have the last word in death—and a negative one, at that.

At first the appearance of the stone belies the inscription; on top of the stone for George P. Spencer, who died in 1908, is the image of a small child sleeping with his head on a pillow. Right below the figure, an inscription reads:

A DREAMLESS SLEEP, EMBLEM OF ETERNAL REST.

Then the fireworks begin. Spencer was a lifelong atheist who publicly riled churchgoers in Lyndon Center by challenging them on the existence of God. Some may have breathed a sigh of relief at his passing, but Spencer, who was eighty-three when he died, was a stonecutter by trade, so he not only designed and carved his own stone but also carved the letters so deep that he clearly anticipated his former neighbors trying—in vain—to rub the inscription off. It reads, in part:

BEYOND THE UNIVERSE THERE IS NOTHING AND WITHIN THE UNIVERSE THE
SUPERNATURAL DOES NOT EXIST. . . . SCIENCE HAS NEVER KILLED OR PERSE-
CUTED A SINGLE PERSON FOR DOUBTING OR DENYING ITS TEACHINGS, AND
MOST OF THESE TEACHINGS HAVE BEEN TRUE; BUT RELIGION HAS MURDERED
MILLIONS FOR DOUBTING OR DENYING HER DOGMAS, AND MOST OF THESE
DOGMAS HAVE BEEN FALSE.

Given these views, one wonders how he managed to make a living as a stonecarver if the majority of his work consisted of carving inscriptions for his pious neighbors. And what of the sleeping child on the stone? One can only assume that because of his line of work, he got a deep discount. That, or he wanted to continue to anger his neighbors in death as he did in life.

CIVIL WAR HORSE GRAVE

Monument to a Horse

MENDON

Public cemetery

North side of Route 4.
Grounds open dawn to dusk.

This isn't exactly a cemetery, but it warrants a mention anyway due to its unique quality.

Just east of Rutland, the town of Mendon contains an unusual monument that thousands of people pass by every day without even knowing it's there. Once you cross the border into Mendon from Rutland on Route 4 East, pull into the parking lot of the Sugar and Spice Restaurant. Park in the far lot and look for the biggest rock in the forest to the right of the sugar shack. Most days, there's a tiny American flag flying on top. This is Mendon's Civil War Horse Monument. The inscription on the concave section of the rock reads:

THE GRAVE OF GENERAL EDWARD RILEY'S OLD JOHN—GALLANT WAR HORSE
OF THE GREAT CIVIL WAR 1861–1865.

General Edward Ripley was the commander of the Union forces occupying Richmond, Virginia, during the Civil War, in addition to being the commander of the Ninth Vermont Volunteer Infantry. Mendon served as his home when he wasn't at war or traveling with his contingent.

There's a picnic table nearby for an informal meal, or you can sit atop the rock for a bird's-eye view of the traffic going by on the highway. Just don't sit up there after it's been raining—it can be pretty slippery.

WEST CEMETERY

Mummy Dearest

MIDDLEBURY

Public cemetery

*From downtown Middlebury, head south on Route
30 for about 1 mile; the cemetery is on the right.
Grounds open dawn to dusk.*

In Middlebury, when you see a tombstone in West Cemetery where the
date of death is listed as 1883 B.C., it's hard not to wonder what kind
of prank the carver must have been playing when he was working on
that stone.

Believe it or not, the carver was telling the stone-cold truth: The
person buried beneath the marker did actually die in that year and that
era. The deceased is actually an Egyptian mummy whose real name was
Amun-Her-Khepesh-Ef, the young son of an actual Egyptian king. The
route the mummy took to reach Middlebury had to be pretty round-
about, but the best that local historians can figure is that a man named

All Tangled Up

SOON AFTER A NEANDERTHAL MAN OR WOMAN DIED,
THE BODY WAS FOLDED UP INTO A FETAL POSITION AND
TIED UP WITH CORD. THEY MAY HAVE THOUGHT THAT
THE MORE THE DEAD LOOK LIKE THEY'RE SLEEPING,
THE BETTER CHANCE THEY HAVE TO WAKE UP.

Henry Sheldon, one of Middlebury's junk dealers, purchased the mummy from an antiques dealer in New York in the early 1900s. Sheldon kept it in his house until he died, at which point a museum was founded to display all the "stuff" that he had accumulated during his life. The mummy was discovered, and after debating what to do with it, the board of the museum decided that the best option was to bury the mummy in a local graveyard.

George Mead, president of the board, took it upon himself to bring the mummy to a local mortuary for cremation and then placed the ashes in his family's burial plot in West Cemetery. Mystery solved.

GREEN MOUNT CEMETERY

A Dog and a Fire Hydrant

MONTPELIER

Public cemetery

From downtown Montpelier, take Route 2 west
for 2 miles; the cemetery is on the right.
Grounds open dawn to dusk.

Some taphophiles feel that Green Mount Cemetery gets a bum rap, simply due to its proximity to Hope Cemetery in Barre, one town over. Admittedly, Green Mount is rarely touted as a tourist attraction or historic site by the appropriate state government agencies. This is a shame, because Green Mount Cemetery—not to be confused with the one-word Greenmount Cemetery north in Burlington—presents numerous examples of detailed, poignant statuary that rival the monuments in the much larger Hope Cemetery a short drive away.

For one, even though the yard is not a pet cemetery, it has numerous animal statues on the grounds. One is for Ned the Dog, who belonged to a man named Fred Stevens, whose grave is located just behind Ned's realistic statue.

A few graves over from Ned the Dog is undoubtedly the cemetery's most famous statue, however: that of Margaret Pitkin, a young girl who died in 1899. The statue features great detail and shows the girl standing up, leaning on part of a wooden fence with lilies planted near each post. Her dress is intricately carved in the fashion of the day, and she rests her chin in her hand, looking poignantly out at the hills.

Near the entrance of the cemetery is the statue of Joel Foster, who directed the city's waterworks program for many years. Foster died in

"Stairs to Nowhere," a memorial to
W. A. Stowell

1903 at the age of seventy-eight, and as one way to thank him, the city
government paid a local stonecutter to create a life-sized statue of the
man, complete with derby hat and fire hydrant, which he leans on. And
of course you'll notice the "Stairs to Nowhere," a hulking granite staircase carved out of granite lodged in the side of a hill in the graveyard.
The staircase serves as the memorial for a man named W. A. Stowell, as
depicted on a plaque embedded in the hillside.

EVERGREEN CEMETERY

A Window into the Soul?

NEW HAVEN

Public cemetery

Just west of the village of New Haven on Route 17, turn south onto Town Hill Road. The cemetery is 0.5 mile down on your left. Grounds open dawn to dusk.

In the nineteenth century, while death was of course common, it was also very much misunderstood. Stories about people being accidentally buried alive—when others verified by a glance that they were indeed dead—were passed around with abandon.

As a result, a veritable cottage industry developed to ensure that if a person were indeed buried alive, a contraption would help alert the living to this tragic mistake so they could hasten to extricate the unfortunate body from the ground before it was too late. One such item included a series of pulleys and strings that ran from the inside of the casket to the outside of the grave and ultimately to a bell. If the "corpse" awoke, the bell would ring, and the family could be alerted.

Of course, as a body decomposes it naturally moves anyway, which would create a series of false alarms, so people eventually learned to rely on the three-day "wake" to prove that a body was destined for the burying ground. A supplementary tool was a small pocket mirror to hold in front of the deceased's mouth, to see if it would fog up.

Timothy Clark Smith of New Haven, Vermont, didn't trust any of it. He arranged for the cemetery sexton to create a massive mound of earth that would serve as Mister Smith's final resting place, but he wanted a guarantee that he wouldn't be buried alive. The grave, in front of the cemetery between the ENTRANCE and EXIT signs, was constructed so that a pane of glass was situated directly over his face in the casket. Then a cement tube ran from the casket up through the earth to the surface; on that end, another piece of plate glass was set, so in the early days of his interment, passersby could look in the tube down into the earth and see—and supposedly also hear—if the man was screaming, "Let me out!"

However, this was also in the days before flashlights, and no mention was made of how long the cement tube ran—presumably, it had to be at least 6 feet long. In any case, despite his invention, Smith wasn't taking any chances: He instructed his burial cortege to place a bell in his hand so he could ring it in case he really wasn't dead. Again, since the bell was on the inside of a heavily padded casket and underneath several tons of dirt, it seems that he may have overlooked a few things, but no matter. If Mister Smith were alive today, he'd be happy to discover that yes, he was really dead.

ST. MARY'S CEMETERY

A Lengthy Civil War Journey

NEWPORT

Public cemetery

*From downtown Newport, head south on
Route 5 for about 1 mile. Make a sharp left onto
Prospect Street; the cemetery is on the right.
Grounds open dawn to dusk.*

Vermont sent many of her sons off to war, and inevitably, when they boarded the train or carriage that would carry them off to battle, it was the last time that some of them would set foot on Vermont soil, dead or alive.

Indeed, particularly as a result of some of the Civil War's bloodiest battles, many of the bodies of killed soldiers were dumped in mass graves near the battlefield, simply because in many cases it was the only way to deal with the sheer carnage in the heat of summer.

Tom Dunn, a great-grandnephew of John Dunn, a private who served with the Third Vermont Regiment and was killed in action in 1864, always thought it was wrong that no monument to his great-granduncle had ever been erected, despite the fact that his body was never found or returned to his family in Newport, Vermont. In fact, Tom Dunn conducted extensive research among local churches and cemeteries around Newport to see if the body had been shipped to any of these establishments, but he found no proof.

So he decided to take matters into his own hands, and he contacted the Veterans Administration to see if they would provide the family with a memorial stone, which the family felt was the very least

Better late than never: In 1999 a stone
was dedicated to a Civil War soldier
assumed dead in 1864.

that could be done. A family member had already generously donated
a burial lot at St. Mary's Cemetery in Newport. Tom Dunn provided
details of his research into his great-granduncle's life and service and
filled out an application. The VA approved his request, and several
months later the headstone arrived in Newport and was set up in the
cemetery.

The dedication of the stone, on August 21, 1999, was extremely
touching for the family. A contingent from a group of Civil War re-
enactors showed up to offer an authentic military sendoff for John
Dunn, complete with vintage muskets and march.

NOTCH CEMETERY

Grave Site of Calvin Coolidge

PLYMOUTH

Public cemetery

*Route 100A, adjacent to the Calvin Coolidge
Birthplace. Grounds open dawn to dusk.*

Calvin Coolidge, whose nickname was "Silent Cal" due to his typical Vermonter's gift of not saying anything when there wasn't anything to say, was one of the two presidents born in Vermont. His birthplace, which is today a state historic site, features his boyhood home and the actual table and kerosene lamp present when then Vice President Coolidge was given the oath of office by his father (a notary public) upon hearing of President Warren G. Harding's death.

In the Notch Cemetery nearby, where Coolidge and his wife are buried, the former first family's tombstones are similarly plain. Given the president's nature, it's fitting that his headstone contains no epitaph, though it does have the presidential seal inscribed into the marker. Some historians note that Coolidge was often compared to Abraham Lincoln in terms of the ability to rise above relatively simple backgrounds, but when it came to personal accomplishments, Coolidge couldn't distinguish himself, which is why he served only one full term after fulfilling the remainder of Harding's term.

Still, in this corner of Vermont, Coolidge was the biggest thing to ever come down the pike. The stretch of Route 100 that runs from Route 100A in Plymouth to Route 103 in Ludlow is known as the Calvin Coolidge Memorial Highway. The thirtieth president would probably be dismayed to learn of the thousands of cars that travel the

Designers of Vermont cemeteries often had no choice but
to follow the mountainous landscape.

route during a typical winter weekend day when nearby ski resorts are bustling, but in the cemetery and Silent Cal's home, it feels like time has stood still.

The stone for Calvin "Silent Cal"
Coolidge has, fittingly, no epitaph.

RANDOLPH CENTER CEMETERY

A Horse Is a Horse, Of Course

RANDOLPH

Public cemetery

On Route 12, across from Vermont Technical College. Grounds open dawn to dusk.

Vermont, like other New England states, has more than its fair share of legends. In the Green Mountain State, however, there seem to be more stories that are heartwarming and poignant than you'll find in the five other states. Or it could just be that the air is different.

In any case, the story of how the Morgan horse ended up as the official Vermont State Animal is appropriately touching. A man by the name of Justin Morgan was a teacher in Massachusetts, and he made his living by giving private lessons in both singing and penmanship. He was relatively footloose while practicing his profession, but in 1789, when he was about forty-two years old, it seems that he grew tired of living on the road, so he accepted the position of town clerk in the central Vermont town of Randolph.

As he traveled north to his new home, he continued to give lessons, but when it came time to pay, one student had no money. Instead, he offered a small two-year-old horse to Morgan. Though the teacher wouldn't need it in his new position, he accepted the horse anyway and brought it with him to Vermont. There, despite his size, the chestnut-brown horse astounded the townspeople with his strength. Word traveled, and though Morgan ended up dying several years later, some of the locals took on the care of the little horse—which Morgan had named Figure—and proceeded to breed him and spread word of the hardworking animal they'd named after their town clerk.

Today the Morgan Horse Farm, located in Middlebury, Vermont, is where the descendants of Morgan's first horse live, and the farm is associated with the University of Vermont. Justin Morgan himself is buried in his adopted town of Randolph. His tombstone, in the northwest corner of the Randolph Center Cemetery, reads:

THIS MAN BROUGHT TO VERMONT THE COLT FROM WHICH ALL MORGAN
HORSES ARE DESCENDED.

The High Cost of Dying

FOLLOWING THE DROWNING DEATH OF AN
EIGHTEENTH-CENTURY NEW ENGLAND MAN, THE
FOLLOWING WAS ORDERED TO PAY PEOPLE WHO
HAD ASSISTED IN HIS FUNERAL:

BUY A PINT OF LIQUOR FOR THOSE
WHO DIVED FOR HIM.
BUY A QUART OF LIQUOR FOR THOSE
WHO BROUGHT HIM HOME.
BUY TWO QUARTS OF WINE AND ONE GALLON
OF CIDER TO JURY OF INQUEST.
BUY 8 GALLONS AND 3 QUARTS WINE FOR FUNERAL.
BUY BARREL OF CIDER FOR FUNERAL.

THE GESTURE, AND THE AMOUNTS, WERE TYPICAL
OF THE DAY.

BEN & JERRY'S
FLAVOR GRAVEYARD

Where the Old Flavors Live

WATERBURY

*On the grounds of the factory store on Route 100.
Grounds open dawn to dusk. (802) 882–1240;
www.benandjerrys.com.*

You know what Ben & Jerry's is all about: great ice cream flavors. And you may have been miffed at them at some time in the past due to the fact that all of a sudden you couldn't find your favorite flavor in any of the usual places.

In fact, you may have been so miffed that you even called up the headquarters in Waterbury, Vermont, and asked to speak to Ben or Jerry so you could register your displeasure.

Over the years the company must have gotten tired of hearing from irate customers who were enraptured by a particular flavor—perhaps Ice Tea with Ginseng, or Kiwi Midori—only to learn that nobody else liked it. And so to appease the five people in the universe who will never again have Peanut Butter & Jelly ice cream rolling around on their tongues, Ben and Jerry came up with the Flavor Graveyard at their main factory in Waterbury. Each of the twenty-six flavors (as of this writing) in the "cemetery" has its own stone with a fitting, rhyming epitaph. The picture on each headstone shows an ice cream cone that's grown wings and is on its way, presumably, to ice cream heaven.

Here's one:

On a lighter note: Ben & Jerry's Flavor Graveyard

HOLY CANNOLI
NOW IN FRONT OF THE PEARLY GATES,
HOLY CANNOLI SITS AND WAITS.
WHAT BROUGHT ITS RUIN NO ONE KNOWS,
MUST HAVE BEEN THE PISTACHIOS.
1997–1998

And another:

PEANUTS! POPCORN!
PEANUTS, POPCORN!
MIX 'EM IN A POT!
PLOP 'EM IN YOUR ICE CREAM!
WELL, MAYBE NOT.
2000–2000

Hopefully the deceased ice creams were at least better than the verse on the stones. The sad part is that they don't give any warning when they're about to yank a flavor, so you don't know when to stock up.

Due to the popularity of its Flavor Graveyard on the factory premises, the company has also added a flavor graveyard interactive game at its Web site, www.benandjerrys.com, in case you can't visit the real thing, or you go through withdrawal after having visited the real thing in person. There's even a form you can fill out to beg, plead, and grovel for your flavor to return, or perhaps to suggest a new one, which may, after all, end up featured in the Flavor Graveyard, both real and virtual.

Appendix A

Common Symbols on Gravestones

If you visit enough old New England cemeteries, you'll see a variety of signs and symbols inscribed into the gravestones and markers. Here are brief translations for the most common symbols you'll spot:

Acanthus leaves—Life everlasting
Anchor or ships—Christian hope; seafaring profession
Angel, flying—Rebirth; resurrection
Angel, trumpeting—Resurrection
Angel, weeping—Grief and mourning
Arch—Victory in death
Arrow—Mortality
Bible—Revelation and salvation
Bird—Eternal life
Bird, flying—Resurrection; flight of the soul
Book—The Bible
Breasts, gourds, or pomegranates—Nourishment of the soul; the church
Bouquets or flowers—Condolences; grief; sorrow
Broken column—Loss of the head of a family
Broken ring—Family circle severed
Buds or rosebud—Morning of life or renewal of life
Bugles—Resurrection; the military
Butterfly—Short-lived; an early death
Candle being snuffed—Time; mortality
Cherub—Angelic
Cock—Vigilance; fall from grace
Coffin, Father Time, picks and shovels, darts—Mortality

Columns and doors—Heavenly entrance

Coiled snake or rope—Eternal life

Corn—Ripe old age

Cross—Faith

Crossed swords—High-ranking military person

Crown—Glory of life after death

Cup or chalice—The sacraments

Dove—Purity; devotion

Dove, flying—Resurrection

Drapes—Mourning; mortality

Flame or light—Life; resurrection

Flower—Fragility of life

Flower, severed stem—Shortened life

Fruits—Eternal plenty

Full-blown rose—Prime of life

Garland or wreath—Victory in death

Grapevine—Church is the vine, members are the grapes

Grim Reaper—Death personified

Hand, pointing up—Pathway to heaven; heavenly reward

Hands, clasped—The good-byes said at death

Hand of God chopping—Sudden death

Handshakes—Farewell

Harp—Praise to the Maker

Heart—Love; love of God; abode of the soul; mortality

Horns—The resurrection

Hourglass—Passing of time

Hourglass, flying—Time flies

Imps—Mortality

Ivy—Friendship and immortality

Lamb—Innocence

Laurel—Fame or victory

Lily or lily of valley—Innocence and purity

Lion—Courage; the Lion of Judah

Moon, stars, sun—Soul rising to heaven

Morning glory—Beginning of life

Oak leaves and acorn—Maturity; ripe old age
Open book or Bible—Deceased teacher, minister, etc.
Pall—Mortality
Palm branch—Victory and rejoicing
Pick—Death; mortality
Pointing hand—Emblem of God
Poppy—Sleep
Portals—Passageway to eternal journey
Rod or staff—Comfort for the bereaved
Rooster—Awakening; resurrection
Roses—Brevity of earthly existence
Scallop shell—Humankind's earthly pilgrimage
Scythe—Death; the divine harvest
Seashell—Resurrection; life everlasting; life's pilgrimage
Sheaf of Wheat—Ripe for harvest; divine harvest; time
Skull, skeleton, bones—Mortality; death
Skeleton—Life's brevity
Snake, tail in mouth—Everlasting life in heaven
Spade—Mortality; death
Stars and stripes around eagle—Eternal vigilance; liberty
Sun rising—Renewed life
Sun shining—Life everlasting
Sun setting—Death
Thistle—Scottish descent
Thistles—Remembrance
Tombs—Mortality
Torch, inverted—Life extinct
Tree—Life
Tree, sprouting—Life everlasting
Tree, severed branch—Mortality
Tree stump—Life interrupted
Tree stump with ivy—Head of family; immortality
Tree trunk—Brevity of life
Tree trunk, leaning—Short, interrupted life
Trumpeting figure—Herald of the resurrection

Urn—Immortality (ancient Egyptians believed that life would be
    restored in the future through placing the vital organs in an urn)
Urn with wreath or crepe—Mourning
Urn with blaze—Undying friendship
Weeping willow tree—Mourning; grief; nature's lament
Willows—Earthly sorrow
Winged cherub—Resurrected immortal soul
Winged face—Effigy of the deceased soul; the soul in flight
Winged skull—Flight of the soul from mortals
Wreath—Victory
Wreath on skull—Victory of death over life
Wheat strands or sheaves—The divine harvest

APPENDIX B

Common Abbreviations on Gravestones

Besides the carved symbols and pictures you'll see on many old gravestones in New England cemeteries, you'll also witness a bewildering array of abbreviations that almost seem like Latin. They are acronyms for a variety of fraternal organizations and are deciphered here:

AAONMS—Ancient Arabic Order of Nobles of the Mystic
   Shrine (Masonic)
AASR—Ancient and Accepted Scottish Rite (Masonic)
ABA—American Benefit Association
AF&AM—Ancient Free and Accepted Masons
ALOH—American Legion of Honor
AMD—Allied Masonic Degree
AMORC—Ancient and Mystical Order Rosae Crucis (Rosicrucians)
AMOS—Ancient Mystic Order of Samaritans (see IOOF)
AOF—Ancient Order of Foresters
AOH—Ancient Order of Hibernians
AOKMC—Ancient Order of Knights of Mystic Chain
AOUW—Ancient Order of United Workmen
APA—American Protective Association
AUM—Ancient Order of Mysteries (Masonic)
AUSA—Association of the United States Army
AUV—Association of Union Veterans

BARE—Benefit Association of Railway Employees
BAY—Brotherhood of American Yeomen
BKA—Benevolent Knights Association

BK of M—Black Knights of Molders
BLE—Brotherhood of Locomotive Engineers
BLF&E—Brotherhood of Locomotive Firemen and Engineers
B of RTM—Brotherhood of Rail Road Track Men
BPOE—Benevolent and Protective Order of Elks
BPOEW—Benevolent and Protective Order of Elks of the World
BRT—Brotherhood of Railway Trainmen

CAR—Children of the American Revolution
CBKA—Commandery Benevolent Knights Association
CBL—Catholic Benevolent Legion
CCTAS—Crusaders-Catholic Total Abstinence Society
CD of A—Catholic Daughters of America
CK of A—Catholic Knights of America
CMBA—Catholic Mutual Benefit Association
COOF—Catholic Order of Foresters
CSA—Confederate States Army
CTAS—Catholic Total Abstinence Society

DAC—Daughters of the American Colonists
DAR—Daughters of the American Revolution
DAV—Disabled American Veterans
D.O.A./DA—Daughters of America
DOKK—Dramatic Order Knights of Khorassan (Knights of Pythias)
DoL—Daughters of Liberty
DOLLUS—Dames of the Loyal Legion of the United States
DON—Daughters of the Nile (Masonic)
DUV—Daughters of Union Veterans of the Civil War

EAA—Experimental Aircraft Association
EAU—Equitable Aid Union
EBA—Emerald Beneficial Association

FAA—Free and Accepted Americans
FAM—Free and Accepted Masons

FCB—Knights of Pythias
FLT—Independent Order of Odd Fellows
FMF—Fleet Marine Force
FOAST—Fraternal Order of Alaska State Troopers
FOE—Fraternal Order of Eagles
FOF—Fraternal Order of Firefighters
FOP—Fraternal Order of Police

GALSTPTR—German American Legion of St. Peter
GAR—Grand Army of the Republic
GLAUM—Grand Lodge Ancient Order of Mysteries—Masonic Order
GLDS—Grand Lodge Daughters of Scotia
GUOOF—Grand United Order of Odd Fellows

IBBH—International Brotherhood of Blacksmiths and Helpers
ICBU—Irish Catholic Benevolent Union
IHSV—Red Cross of Constantine (Masonic)
IOA—International Order of Alhambra
IODE—Independent Order, Daughters of the Empire
IOF—Independent Order of Foresters
IOI—Independent Order of Immaculates
IOJD—Independent Order of Job's Daughters
IOKP—Independent Order of Knights of Pythias
IOOF—Independent Order of Odd Fellows
IOOF-PM—Independent Order of Odd Fellows, Past Master
IORG—International Order of Rainbow Girls (Masonic)
IORM—Improved Order of Redmen (Sons of Liberty)
IOStL—Independent Order of St. Luke
IOV—International Order of Vikings
ISDA—Italian Sons and Daughters of America
ISH—Independent Sons of Honor
IUOM—Independent United Order of Mechanics
IWW—Industrial Workers of the World

JAOUW—Junior Order—Ancient Order of United Workmen
J.O.A.M.—Junior Order of American Mechanics
J.O.U.A.M.—Junior Order of United American Mechanics

KC—Knights of Columbus
KFM—Knights of Father Matthew
KG—Knights of St. George
KGC—Knights of the Golden Chain; Knights of the Golden Circle
KGE—Knights of the Golden Eagle
KGL—Knight Grand Legion
KHC—Knights of Holy Cross
KKK—Knights of Ku Klux Klan
KLH—Knights and Ladies of Honor
KM—Knights Militant (see KKK); Knights of Malta (Masonic)
KMC—Knights of the Mystic Chain
K. of C.—Knights of Columbus
K of FM—Knights of Father Matthew
K of H—Knights of Honor
K of L—Knights of Loyola
K. of P.—Knights of Pythias
K of SJ—Knights of St. John
K of STP—Knights of St. Patrick
K of STW—Knights of St. Wenceslas
K of T—Knights of Tabor
K of TM—Knights of the Maccabees
KOL—Knights of Labor
KOTM—Knights of the Maccabees
KP—Knights of Pythias
KSL—Knights of St. Lawrence
KSTG—Knights of St. George
KSTI—Knights of St. Ignatius
KSTJ—Knights of St. Joseph
KSTM—Knights of St. Martin
KSTP—Knights of St. Paul; Knights of St. Peter
KSTT—Knights of St. Thomas

KT—Knights of Tabor; Knights Templars (Masonic)

LAOH—Ladies Ancient Order of Hibernians
LDG—Independent Order of Foresters
LGAR—Ladies of the Grand Army of the Republic
LK of A—Loyal Knights of America
L.O.M, LOOM—Loyal Order of Moose
LOVUS—Legion of Valor of the United States

MAW—Marine Air Wing
MBS—Mutual Benefit Society
MCL—Marine Corps League
MOLLUS—Military Order of the Loyal Legion of the United States
MOOSE—Loyal Order of the Moose
MOPH—Military Order of the Purple Heart
MRA—Royal Arcanum
M.W.A.—Modern Woodmen of America

NCOA—Non-Commissioned Officers Association (Military Society)
NEOP—New England Order of Protection
NL—Navy League
NOK—New Order Knights (see KKK)
N.O.W.—Neighbors of Woodcraft
NSDAR—National Society Daughters of the American Revolution
NSSUP—National Society Sons of Utah Pioneers
NU—National Union

OCF—Order of Chosen Friends
OES—Order of the Eastern Star
OGC—Order of the Golden Cross
O of A—Order of Amaranth (Masonic)
O of UF—Order of United Friends
OSC—Order of Scottish Clans (St. Andrew's Societies)
OUAM—Order of United American Mechanics

PF of A—Patriotic Friends of America
PH—The Order of Patrons of Husbandry (The Grange)
PM—Patriarchs Militant (Independent Order of Odd Fellows)

RA—Royal Academy; Royal Arcanum
R.A.M.—Royal Arch Masons
RIP—*Requiescat in pace,* Latin for "Rest in peace"
RK—Roman Knights
RMOKHSJ—The Religious and Military Order of Knights of the
    Holy Sepulchre of Jerusalem
R.N.A.—Royal Neighbors of America
RO-AUM—Rosicrucian Order (Masonic)
ROJ—Royal Order of Jesters (Masonic)
RSGF—Royal Society of Good Fellows
RSM—Royal and Select Masons
RSTV—Rite of St. Vita
RTT—Royal Templars of Temperance

S.A.L.—Sons of the American Legion
SAR—Sisters of the American Revolution; Sons of the
    American Revolution
S.A.W.V.—Spanish-American War Veteran
SBL—Society B. Lafayette
SCV—Sons of the Confederate Veterans
S.C.V.C.W.—Sons of the Confederate Veterans of the Civil War
S.F.W.C.—Supreme Forest Woodmen Circle
SMAA—Scandinavian Mutual Aid Association
SNA-AUM—Shrine of North America (Masonic)
S.O.C.V.—Sons of the Confederate Veterans
S of E—Sons of England
SR—Scottish Rite (Masonic)
S.S.M.A.—Soldiers and Sailors Memorial Association
ST—Sons of Temperance
ST.G S o NY—St. George's Society of New York
SUVCW or S.U.V.C.W.—Sons of Union Veterans of the Civil War

SV—Sons of Veterans; Sons of Veterans of the United
  States of America

TCL—Tall Cedars of Lebanon (Masonic)
TH—Temple of Honor and Temperance—Independent Order of Odd
  Fellows; Temple of Honor—Independent Order of Odd Fellows
TPLF—Temple of Honor and Temperance, IOOF
TROA—The Retired Officer's Association

UAOD—United Ancient Order of Druids
UCV—United Confederate Veterans
UDC—United Daughters of the Confederacy
UFL—Union Fraternal League
UFM—United Friends of Michigan
UOPF—United Order of Pilgrim Fathers
U.S.A.—United States Army
U.S.A.F.—United States Air Force
U.S.M.C.—United States Marine Corps
U.S.N.—United States Navy

VFW—Veterans of Foreign Wars

W.C.—Woodmen Circle
WKSC—White Knights of the Southern Cross (see KKK)
W.O.W.—Woodmen of the World; Women of Woodcraft

YMCA—Young Men's Christian Association
YWCA—Young Women's Christian Association

BIBLIOGRAPHY

Benes, Peter. *The Masks of Orthodoxy*. Amherst: University of Massachusetts Press, 1977.

Blanchard, Fessenden S. *Ghost Towns of New England: Their Ups and Downs*. New York: Dodd, Mead & Company, 1960.

Carmack, Sharon DeBartolo. *Your Guide to Cemetery Research*. Cincinnati: Betterway Books, 2002.

DiAndrea, Phyllis. *Rubbing Off History: A Guide to New England Gravestones*. Watertown, MA: Self-published, 1975.

Duval, Francis Y., and Ivan B. Rigby. *Early American Gravestone Art in Photographs*. New York: Dover Publications, 1978.

Felsen, Gregg. *Tombstones: Seventy-Five Famous People and Their Final Resting Places*. Berkeley, CA: Ten Speed Press, 1996.

Forbes, Harriette. *Early New England Gravestones and the Men Who Made Them*. Cambridge, MA: Riverside Press, 1927.

George, Diana Hume, and Malcolm A. Nelson. *Epitaph and Icon: A Field Guide to the Old Burial Grounds of Cape Cod*. Orleans, MA: Parnassus Imprints, 1983.

Gillon, Vincent. *Early New England Gravestone Rubbings*. New York: Dover Publications, 1966.

Halporn, Roberta. *Lessons from the Dead: The Graveyard as a Classroom for the Study of the Life Cycle*. Brooklyn, NY: Highly Specialized Promotions, 1979.

Jackson, Kenneth T. *Silent Cities: The Evolution of the American Cemetery*. New York: Princeton Architectural Press, 1989.

Kull, Andrew. *New England Cemeteries: A Collector's Guide.* Brattleboro, VT: Stephen Greene Press, 1975.

Ludwig, Allan. *Graven Images: New England Stonecarving and Its Symbols.* Middletown, CT: Wesleyan University Press, 1966.

Meyer, Richard E., ed. *Cemeteries and Gravemarkers: Voices of American Culture.* Ann Arbor, MI: UMI Research Press, 1989.

Schafer, Louis S. *Best of Gravestone Humor.* New York: Sterling Publishing Company, 1990.

Sloane, David Charles. *The Last Great Necessity: Cemeteries in American History.* Baltimore: Johns Hopkins University Press, 1991.

Smillie, James. *Rural Cemeteries of America.* New York: R. Martin, 1847.

Tashjian, Ann, and Dickran Tashjian. *Memorials for Children of Change: The Art of Early New England Stonecarving.* Middletown, CT: Wesleyan University Press, 1974.

RESOURCES

There are a wealth of organizations and publications out there to help ease the way for New England taphophiles. Whether you are interested in restoring gravestones, cleaning up cemeteries, or researching a particular cemetery, here are some resources to get you started:

Ancestry.com
www.ancestry.com

Association for Gravestone Studies
278 Main Street, Suite 207
Greenfield, MA 01301
413–772–0836
www.gravestonestudies.org

Cape Cod Gravestones
www.capecodgravestones.com
This site offers information on seventeenth-, eighteenth-, and nineteenth-century gravestones in Barnstable County, Massachusetts.

Cemetery Junction
www.daddezio.com/cemetery/index.html

Cemetery Records Online
www.interment.net

Cemetery Photos
www.rootsweb.com/~cemphoto

Cemetery Preservation
www.potifos.com/cemeteries.html

City of the Silent
www.alsirat.com/silence/index.html

Civil War Cemeteries
www.cwc.lsu.edu/cwc/links/hist.htm#Cemeteries

Connecticut Gravestone Network
www.ctgravestones.com

Cyndi's List
www.cyndislist.com/cemetery.htm

Find a Grave
www.findagrave.com

Genealogy Cemetery Sites
www.geneasearch.com/cemeteries.htm

Grave-L
groups.yahoo.com/group/Grave-L
Grave-L is the original list for taphophiles (literally "lovers of tomb-stones"). It focuses primarily on the sociological, anthropological, historical, artistic, spiritual, folkloric, and other nonmorbid aspects of cemeteries and sepulchral culture.

Haunted Cemeteries
www.zerotime.com/ghosts/cemet.htm

Headstone Hunter
http://Headstonehunter.com

HomeTownLocator
http://gazetteer.hometownlocator.com

The Gazetteer at HomeTownLocator.com is an extremely useful resource to search for the exact locations of cemeteries not featured in this book. From the home page, click on "Browse Physical Features and Cultural Features." Select the state you want, then click on "Features," followed by "Cemetery." Each listing includes the cemetery's exact longitude and latitude.

I Dream of Genealogy
www.idreamof.com/

Maine Old Cemetery Association
P.O. Box 641
Augusta, ME 04332
www.rootsweb.com/~memoca/moca.htm

New Hampshire Old Cemetery Association
www.nhcemetery.org

Saving Graves
www.savinggraves.com

Tomb with a View
http://members.aol.com/TombView/twav.html

Tombstone Transcription Project
www.rootsweb.com/~cemetery/index.html

Tombstones & Monument Inscriptions
http://gye.future.easyspace.com/

Vermont Old Cemetery Association
www.sover.net/~hwdbry/voca/

Virtual Cemetery
www.genealogy.com/vcem_welcome.html

INDEX

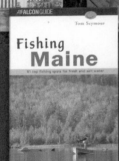